Exploring Wicca

**From the Cauldron to the Altar:
Understanding the Beliefs and
Practices of Wicca**

Isabella Hughes

Table of Contents

INTRODUCTION

One of the most misconstrued yet, by far-very enlightening spiritual paths in use today is wiccan practice. Wicca, an ancient practice with solid bonds to nature, provides its practitioners with a path of harmony, self-determination, and reverence for the planet and all living organisms. What, though, is Wicca just? Religiosity, witchcraft, or something altogether else?

This book, "Exploring Wicca: From the Cauldron to the Altar: Understanding the Beliefs and Practices of Wicca," brings us into the heart of Wicca, shedding light on the rite, spiritual practices, and believes. But this is not only an introduction but also a guide for the Wiccan novice. Here are all the main ideas that cover the core of Wicca, its gods, and its rites. It gives far more depth to the practice of levels of Wiccan spirituality and magical practices for the more mature practitioner.

This book takes you down the core ideas of Wicca-from understanding the dualism of the God and Goddess to exploring the sacred Wheel of the Year. Practical's, spells, and rituals are the living heartbeat of Wicca practice along the path: personal growth, spiritual connection, and deeper understanding of the cycles of nature-into which they perceive this book as opening.

CHAPTER I

Introduction to Wicca

The Roots of Wicca

Wicca is a modern, neo-liturgical religion that stitches together new and creative forms of modern religious expression, folklore, ceremonial magic, and ancient pagan custom. It is the result of hundreds of years of historical developments: elements of pre-Christian belief, European witchcraft traditions, and 19th- and 20th-century revivalist movements. A journey in time is necessary to approach understanding the roots of Wicca. There it is where we find the ancient people religious rituals, persecution of suspected witches in the course of the European witch trials, and, eventually, the esoteric spirituality of early modern times which would ultimately be resurfaced again. All these came to form what is now generally known today as Wicca, a polytheistic nature-based religion following life, death, and rebirth cycles.

Although many attribute the old paganism that covered Europe in the years before Christianity came to the continent, it is itself largely an origin based on history for

Wicca. There were several regional and cultural variants of those paganism, but despite those differences, there were unifying principles to these, which included reverence of the natural world, polytheistic worship of deities, as well as a close connection with the cycles of the seasons. These ancient nomadic tribes believed that gods and goddesses controlled things in life. For instance, they thought the gods controlled fertility and agriculture, weather and death, among other things. For these tribes, natural world was considered to be full of divine presence as well. In fact, many of these gods are linked with sacred places in the natural world-such as rivers, mountains, and woods. This was accomplished through the performances of rituals, which, as believed by people, would please the gods, bring good harvests, and balance nature's factors with each other and themselves. This is evident, for instance, in that developed Celtic spirituality was based on their reverence for the natural world and on the sacred nature of the earth. Celts had their priest, called druids, who were entrusted with giving spiritual directions and offering sacrifices on behalf of the masses and gods. Though the festivals are seasonally based-events to celebrate Samhain, Imbolc, Beltane, and Lughnasadh-they depict the cycle of life and death, which, although a different thing, is celebrated in principal moments within the agro-year. Many such festivals have been adopted by modern Wiccans as parts of the Wheel of the Year, which goes on to prove that the more antique version of paganism is unusually influential in the present.

Besides these vintage religious rituals, the act of witchcraft and its persecution in Europe influenced Wicca considerably. During late Middle Ages and early Modern period, European society began to be more and more alarmed about witches. They defined that witches were the people who practice evil magic and did this in confluence with the devil. At that time, the common belief of good and evil defined Christian thoughts, which led to massive suspicion, violence, and terror. Tens of thousands of people-killing many of whom were women-were killed due to the conducted European witch trials that exploded into the 16th and 17th centuries and accused many more for practicing witchcraft. However, most of the accused witches had no relation to modern paganism or Wicca but, rather, were all too often women who served as midwives, healers, or misfits in their own societies. Still, the view of witches as magicians stuck in the public imagination and would influence the current forms of contemporary Wicca. The definition of modern Wicca in terms of women, magic, and the natural world from which sprang the image of persecution of witches means that this image of a witch as the wise woman who draws upon the forces of nature-in harmony with natural cycles-for healing and spiritual purposes they appropriate, though they do not perceive themselves as those who wield evil.

It was the confluence of Spiritualism, the 19th century, and Romantic movements that together co-raised interest in the occult and mystical esotericism. There came a time when Enlightenment was able to draw out the impact of magical and esoteric thought; it was the age that led the thinking of Romantic writers and thinkers to rekindle enthusiasm for the mysterious, the supernatural, and the antique. This movement was an adoption of independence, natural phenomena, and exploration of old, time-worthy knowledge. That change of culture paved the way for pagan ideas to revive in Europe. Meanwhile, anthropologists and folklorists recorded the leftovers of antiquated pagan practices that were preserved in rural areas, mostly masquerading as folk traditions or Christian rituals. Some folkloric research in several European countries led to the conclusion that there was no destruction but an incorporation of pagan beliefs that dominated before coming Christianity. Such examples include seasonal rites, healing rituals, and veneration of sanctified places.

Of course, among the most prominent 20th-century scholars/occultists, who contributed to the formation of modern Wicca, are Margaret Murray and Aleister Crowley. Published in the 1920s and 1930s, the writings of British Egyptologist and folklorist Margaret Murray, specifically the books, are made to make a point about an underground, secret cult of witches existing in Europe since pre-Christian times. She argues that this witch cult continued ancient fertility religions which worshipped a mother goddess and a horned god with rituals ensuring the fertility of crops and animals. She was most important to the early Wiccan movement, which emphasized that witchcraft was a form in which archaic pagan practices persisted; however, later historians have largely discredited her theory. This doctrine was founded by Aleister Crowley, an influential English occultist and ceremonial magician. His concepts and the methodology of magic in his books ensured that modern paganism and magic often existed in reality in dependence on Gnostic and ancient Egyptian traditions. Much of Crowley's assumptions on ritual magic, invocation of deities, and individual spiritual empowerment formed the foundation for Gerald Gardner, upon which were aptly implemented the magic practice that he was to develop as Wiccan.

Many consider that the whole modern Wicca tradition was founded by a man named Gerald Gardner, who was born in 1884 and was an English civil servant. He was also an amateur anthropologist, as well as a precursory member of an occult, whose interest in this mystical practice, magic, and especially witchcraft led him to take an even deeper interest in them, even while he served the British post-colonial service which took him completely into the whole British occult scene. He was closely associated with the Rosicrucian Order Crotona Fellowship-an organization which was actively sowing the seeds of spiritual practice by deriving traits from both ceremonial magic, Freemasonry and Theosophy. Gardner later claimed that through this organization he had been initiated into a coven of operational witches in the New Forest at the end of the 1930s. He believes that this coven was a continuation of the old witch religion about which Margaret Murray had written, and the kind of witchcraft practiced by its members constitutes paganism that, over the generations, has survived underground.

Gardner continued to write books on witchcraft, the most famous of which is *Witchcraft Today*, published in 1954. In the pages of that book, Gardner revealed the world what he called "the Old Religion," a continuing resurgence of prehistoric pagan beliefs and customs centered around ritual magic, festival celebration, and the worship of a god or goddess. Therefore, ceremonial magic found its space within the Wicca of Gardner in the ritual invocation of deities, casting of ritual circles, and the use of magical objects such as wands and athame. He also has extensively used the books of Crowley, thus generating ideas from his rituals and mystical techniques. Despite that, Wicca, Gardner said, was a nature religion which has been centered upon the cycles of the moon and earth, and harmony between the opposing forces of men and women.

Wicca spread fast within the United Kingdom and across the world following the publication of *Witchcraft Today*. It developed into a prosperous and diverse spiritual movement during the succeeding decades. Other Wiccan traditions were based upon Gardner's Wicca, known as Alexandrian Wicca from Alex Sanders, a student of Gardner and eclectic Wicca, which allows its users to bring together ideas from other traditions and sources. Spiritual liberty, personal experience, and a deep connection with nature resonated in the countercultural movements of the 1960s and 1970s that echoed many of its sentiments.

These are some of the main reasons why people are attracted to Wicca, namely in flexibility and variety in practice. Contrary to most of the religions that may be considered an organized faith, Wicca has no one or more sacred books that direct the followers. Most current Wiccans believe in eclectic Wicca, which takes bits and pieces from other spiritual paths that include Eastern religions, Native American spirituality, as well as other pagan traditions, while Gardnerian Wicca has specific rites and beliefs. Since Wicca is adaptive, it can, therefore be bent to fulfill the needs and preference of some practitioners to satisfy the broad needs of a wide array of practitioners. All the seasonal celebrations, the love for nature, and the practice of magic have wildly associated them with ancient roots, what best describes the most unique characteristic of Wicca is its connection with nature that is also an immediate contact with its ancient past. Since earth is sacred for the Wiccans, many of their rituals are designed to aid the practitioners in being attuned with the cycles of nature. Wiccans celebrate eight periodic celebrations called Sabbats, which are based on the sun's passage throughout the year and the agricultural cycle. These range from solstices and equinoxes to cross-quarter days in between. All festivals symbolize the harmony that ought to exist between God and the Goddess, and mark a specific point in life, death and rebirth. The Goddess, being connected with earth and moon, was considered to be in cycles of fertility, growth, and rebirth; the God, often associated with the sun, was said to be born at Yule, mature at midsummer, and die at Samhain.

The Wiccan practice of Esbats, or full moon rituals aimed at worshiping the Goddess and the cycle of the moon, traces back its roots from ancient pagan customs. The moon has often traditionally represented magic, woman energy, and intuition. Another belief among Wiccans is that the full moon represents a moment of high spiritual energy. For example, in these rituals, which may include spellwork, divination, and meditation, the practitioner tunes themself into the divine feminine and becomes aligned with the cycles of the moon. Magic also forms part of Wicca and has its origins in ancient history. Wiccan belief is that magic is the practice of using one's will and intent to change one's surroundings, typically by tapping into the natural forces, and this concept finds its roots in the folklore and herbalism of olden days and the ceremonial magic of the Renaissance. It perceives magic as a mode of empowerment and transformation in your life by aligning with nature. Most of the presents to gods or the spirits of the ground are well-supported with spells and rituals utilized for healing, protection, love, or self-development reasons.

The Wiccan ethics has its roots in the Wiccan Rede: "An it harm none, do what ye will." It is based on a proper respect for all living things and the direct correlation of its ideas with the natural world. A Wicca devotee is thus called to think before acting in that enhances behaving sensibly and carefully with regard to the influence of one's choices both for the environment and their own selves. The Threefold Law, which claims that whatever amount of energy a person throws into the world-whether it is positive or negative-will return to him threefold adds another reason to personal responsibility ethic.

Wicca is undoubtedly the most confusing and diverse derivation from ancient paganism in its development of European witchcraft and occult revival in the 19th and 20th centuries. Wicca is so unique and interesting a spiritual practice for the contemporary practitioner because it brings to mind an experience with nature, pay respects to the cycles of life, and emphasizes one's spiritual empowerment. Therefore, Wicca remains in evolution and provides its followers with the method of building deep, life-changing relationships with divinity, being in harmony with the natural world, while offering respect for their ancient roots and making space for changes that fulfill the demands of modern society.

Wicca in the Modern World

There is an awareness and impact of wicca in the contemporary world once considered a fringe spiritual activity. Wicca developed from its historical background in 20th-century occultism, witchcraft, and ancient paganism into today's successful spirituality that is recognized and used worldwide, especially in the United States, the United Kingdom, and other English-speaking countries. As the world has increasingly become secular and materialistic, its core principles—reverence for nature, adoration of both masculine and feminine gods, and the practice of ritual and magic to attain spiritual growth—are also spoken to by followers of alternate spirituality. As the world evolves into the twenty-first century, Wicca has developed forms adapted to new and current ideals, including gender equability, environmentalism, and self-autonomy.

It is traced back to the fact that Wicca was an independent religion movement in the 20th century. Its current rise was mainly pushed forward by people like Gerald Gardner, whom many regarded as the father of modern Wicca. The works of Gardner-most importantly, *Witchcraft Today* and *The Meaning of Witchcraft*-popularized the religion in the 1950s. Gardner's Wicca took in elements of folklore, ceremonial magic, and the writings of Margaret Murray-an anthropologist who had insisted that secret pre-Christian witch orders survived for centuries. Although this was nonsense, it later proved entirely false; even at the time it inspired Wicca's mythology as a revival of old pagan ceremonies. Many of the fundamental tenets of modern Wicca, such as seasonal cycles and festivals, the god and goddess, and ceremonial magic, were transplanted to the new world through Gardner. The roots of Wicca had spread so far outward by the 1960s and 1970s that it had fully escaped the United Kingdom. Its rise in the 1960s owes much to the richness of countercultural activism that emphasized individual freedom, environmental consciousness, and alternative spirituality. Wicca drew extensively from a significant number of disillusioned persons who became weary of traditional religions, more particularly those looking forward to a closer, hands-on relationship with God. Wicca's rise also has much to do with the rise of feminism, as women interested in spiritual paths that honored the feminine as holy found Wicca's focus on the Goddess and the sacred feminine appealing.

The Wiccan posture toward nature is one aspect that distinguishes it in modern society. Wicca's lovingness for the natural world and its cycles, on the other hand, provides a spiritual basis for environmental activism in such a time that climate change and environmental degradation are the major global issues. For Wiccans, the land is sacred because nature is a living, breathing animal that deserves respect and protection and not to be dominated or exploited. This concept is characterized by the Wheel of the Year ritual-a holiday that celebrates the changing seasons and agricultural cycles for life. Wiccans have eight seasonal festivals, which are referred to as Sabbats or solstices, equinoxes, and cross-quarter days. Each marks one step in the cycle of life, death, and rebirth. The Wiccan attempts to resonate their spiritual lives to those of the earth by tuning in to such natural cycles.

Although Wheel of the Year is practiced by Wiccans throughout the year, they often perform moon rites known as Esbats. These are performed during full moon and other significant lunar phases. In fact, again, the moon has always been linked to the Goddess in Wicca, who was represented with feminine energy, intuition, and unconscious mysteries long ago. Wiccans can worship the Goddess, hold rituals, and cast spells when gathered in covens or separately at the esbats. Since the moon phases are thought to follow the cycles of life, certain lunar phases are preferable for certain kinds of magical workings according to Wicca. A time for letting go, banishing, and banishment, the waning moon complements the waxing moon with its properties of growth and manifestation. Magic is the main practice of Wicca. More often than not, it is this facet of the religion that has drawn most modern practitioners to it. Magic, to the Wiccan, is the working of one's will and intention to produce some form of change within both worlds-material and spiritual. Wiccans believe that magic is a part of a greater, more pervasive energy in nature that surrounds the universe, and to achieve their intentions, sometimes Wiccans use ritual, visualization, and objects such as candles, herbs, crystals, and symbols. In Wicca philosophy, magic is not seen as a supernatural force but rather as a co-working with the elements of nature to produce change.

The basic ethical teachings underlying Wicca's practice of magic are the words of the Wiccan Rede: "An it harm none, do what ye will." Traditionally, this is interpreted to mean that Wiccans may practice all forms of magic and pursue the dictates of their chosen religious way, so long as they harm no one else. She holds that all acts, magical or mundane, have consequences and adheres to human responsibility: this ethic finds an important base of support in the Threefold Law, stating that whatever energy one sends out into the world—be it positive or negative—returns threefold to oneself. These ethical principles make sure that Wiccans practice magic responsibly, considering human and environmental welfare. Flexibility and acceptance of Wicca are the most prominent features in modern times. Wicca does not have any one holy book, any church head, or dogmas that the followers have to subscribe to, unlike many other organized religions. Instead, Wiccans are told to follow their own spiritual paths and tailor the religion to fit their individual needs and perspectives. Because of its flexibility, Wicca has been able to expand and adapt in the last few decades while absorbing concepts from other religions and evolving to meet new social and cultural demands within the contemporary world. Many modern Wiccans, for example, mix Eastern spirituality into their ritual practice, for example yoga, meditation, and concept of karma. Others take inspiration from indigenous wisdom, particularly in the sense that they may be of such purpose that they want to reach out to their land or to nature.

This is because Wicca, while not mainstream, is decentralized, which is why the popular rising phenomenon is eclectic Wicca-a construction of rituals, practices and beliefs drawing from many different sources. Eclectic wiccan spirituality assists the followers in mixing and combining a number of gods, magical rituals, and spiritual traditions in a manner that it finds importance through its specific beliefs and experiences. Wicca is highly popular with those who cannot fit into the strict norms of more established religions due to its flexibility. It has also opened Wicca to a greater range of people, such as other cultural or ethnic backgrounds, and non-traditionalist gender identities.

Wicca was particularly determined by feminist theory, which still dominates this religion today. Wicca has always highlighted a great emphasis on the Goddess, worshiping and venerating the feminine divine as a source of wisdom, power, and creativity. Countless women who were marginalized or oppressed by patriarchal religious institutions of old find in the sacred feminine an emotional resonance to constitute their own form of Wicca, one in which they can once again assume a role of leadership as priestesses, goddess-like, in service to the feminine divine. Women are exalted in Wicca; other male gods are also worshiped and often believed to have spiritual powers equal to or greater than the authority of men. Much of Wicca ritual and practice is aimed at empowering women by helping them to regain their body, intuition, and bonding to the land.

The modern Wiccan tradition was formed to a large extent by the feminist movement of the 1970s and 1980s, especially with the emergence of feminist Wicca, known sometimes as Dianic Wicca. Zsuzsanna Budapest founded Dianic Wicca, primarily a Goddess-worshipping tradition that is practiced in most cases in covens consisting only of women. Since they believe the Goddess is the origin of all life, Dianic Wiccans focus their rituals on healing, female emancipation, and gaining the spirit power women once had. Even if there are other feminist Wicca traditions, such as Dianic, Dianic Wicca has played a highly significant role in publicizing the Goddess and creating an environment for the deliverance of women from patriarchal idioms of spirituality. Wicca has become not only a space of feminism but has also entered into the realm of LGBTQ+ activism and inclusivity. Because Wicca focuses on the balance of male and female energies and does not identify with rigid gender classification, Wiccans are a diverse group of people in gender identity and orientation. Rituals in most Wiccan traditions focus on the balance of polarities rather than strict male-female opposition. Many worship deities that signify variety in gender manifestations. Many LGBTQ+ people who may have been excluded or marginalized by mainstream religious practices might also identify with Wicca's emphasis on individual freedom and self-empowerment. LGBTQ+ Wiccans have, in recent decades become far more visible in the wider world of Wicca, and many covens visibly welcome LGBTQ+ members.

The general acceptance of Wicca today owes much to the internet. People can now find materials to support their spiritual practices, get in touch with other practitioners and find out more about Wicca than ever before because of online forums and social networking sites as well as websites. Eclectic Wicca has also become more popular due to the internet, through which practitioners can readily communicate their unique rituals, spells, and experiences with people worldwide. As a result, there is now thriving, international Wiccan community where knowledge is shared and the practices can be adapted according to one's beliefs and needs. However, the more popular Wicca becomes, the more the contemporary society sees the disadvantages in it. Due to its popularity, the public and the media sometimes misconstrue or misinterpret Wicca. Witches and Wiccans have been portrayed in many films, serials, and novels that help strengthen the notion of witches being evil or dangerous. Such depictions can spread misconceptions about Wicca, which may result in maltreatment of those who practice it. Despite all these, Wiccans have persisted in advocating a greater understanding and recognition of their belief, averring it to be morally, peaceful, and earth-based in principles.

Wicca is an alive and evolving spiritual way which attracts fresh converts from all walks of society today. For some, a revolutionary inspiration within themselves arises when they relate to the existence of both masculine and feminine elements in divinity, to personal empowerment, and connection with nature-a key essence not found in mainstream religious systems. Wicca is a vibrant, living, and continually evolving religious tradition that allows its adherents to live in harmony with nature, to honor cycles of life, and to produce meaningful, life-changing experiences as it evolves to meet the challenges of twenty-first-century culture, society, and environment.

Wiccan Ethics and Philosophy

Wiccans, like many modern spiritual paths, are governed by a code of morals and doctrines which govern their social, magical, and private lives. Thus, moral precepts are imbedded deep within the religion's respect for the natural world, personal accountability, and harmony and balance. Unlike most of the other major religions, Wicca is not based upon strict rules or precepts. It is instead a very fluid and open-ended theory of morality wherein one's comprehension of her own connection and personal accountability are the bases for moral behavior. Wiccan ethics consist of a general conviction that magic and spirituality are an intrinsic part of everyday existence, as well as the Wiccan Rede and the Threefold Law. The ideals of Wiccans point to intense bonds to the world of nature, equality between the genders, and devotion to one's own spiritual growth.

Perhaps the most famous of Wiccan moral codes is the Wiccan Rede. A common summarized expression of it is: "An it harm none, do what ye will.". One short statement encapsulates the core of Wiccan ethical thought: the freedom to do according to your will, held in check by the duty not to harm another. The Rede is one of the guiding principles for Wiccans, leading them to fully think about what the consequences will be of their acts. In other words, it is not, however, a commandment in the classical sense. It represents the importance of self-autonomy and mutual dependence of all beings. Apart from physical injury, the notion that nothing that person does may harm could also trace its root from emotional, psychological, and environmental impact.

The belief about avoiding harm is grounded from the broader Wiccan perspective that sees life interconnected with one another. Wiccans believe that the universe is made of complex net energies, everything and everyone included in it, and therefore, the actions of one can influence the others and the environment. This holistic view of the world also dictates Wiccan ethics because the practitioners are nudged towards ways of doing things that bring harmony, balance, and healing rather than upsetting or destroying; thus, Wiccan Rede acts both as a reminder of practitioner's duty toward the welfare of the wider world and as a code of morals for personal use. The "do what ye will" principle in the Rede shows that Wiccans do value individual freedom and free choice. In fact, Wicca is a highly autonomous religion that encourages each of its followers to forge their own spiritual pathways and to make their own moral choices. One of the most fundamental tenets of Wicca is the perfect right to do as one pleases, especially as far as magic is concerned. In Wicca religion, magic is the adjustment of the cosmos in accordance with one's will by spells, rituals, or in whatever way possible. The Wiccan Rede offers a moral compass for this activity, urging the wise use of will and even reflection on the effects of one's actions.

The Threefold Law in Wiccan ethics complements this: According to the Threefold Law, one gets back threefold the energy or purpose that they give into the universe, whether this comes about through positive and happy means or ill and negative ways. While the Threefold Law speaks highly of amplifying the acts one makes, this principle of action parallels that of the mechanism of karma for other spiritual traditions. It means that the effect of a person's deed, whether bad or good, will be exaggerated and touch the person but also the entire world. The Threefold Law elevates Wiccans to be good and truthful with accountability through being an effective moral force. It is yet more proof that decisions have long-term implications and such implications are because of one's actions. For instance, in the case of a Wiccan casting a spell to harm another human being, bad energy sent out into the world would return threefold, possibly injuring him or her more seriously. On the other hand, if he or she behaves with love, generosity, or compassion, the Wiccan will receive in abundance everything that person does. The Threefold Law reminds one to act responsibly because one fears punishment in a traditional sense but rather because one knows the law of cause and effect.

Another key concept in Wicca philosophy is balance. For a Wiccan, the universe is the system of changing forces that must be balanced, such as light and dark, life and death, creation and destruction. One of the most common icons is the duality of the God and Goddess, who embody both female and male in a God and Goddess who complement each other in producing and then preserving life. The Wiccans believe in equilibrium as a requirement in the natural world and also in the ethical and spiritual life of an individual. The objective in that regards is balancing with oneself and with the atmosphere around. Equilibrium is also paramount in Wiccan magic practice. Wiccans pay attention, so to speak, to keep the energy they are working with at balance when it comes to performing a ritual or casting a spell. In that case, when one casts a spell for an intention of change, any possible unforeseen consequences should not be overlooked, because, according to Wiccans, magic is neutral energy-not necessarily good or bad-and it's the practitioner who is bound by ethics. Thus, Wiccans are therefore guided to approach their magical work with a sense of vigilance, caution, and serious sense of duty while being always mindful of achieving an affirmative balance between what they intend to achieve and the larger universe at large. Wicca also places equal importance on her relationship with nature and balance. The respect for the environment is one of the major grounds of Wicca as a nature religion. Wiccans believe that everything in this world is connected and that the earth is a sacred land. These beliefs make Wiccans dedicated to environmental stewardship due to their interest in peaceful cohabitation with nature and minimization of individuality in environmental impact. Central to Wiccan practice are notions like sustainability, conservation, and respect for life. Many Wiccans also claim to commit themselves to reverence and care for land through activities of environmental action and activism.

The relationship with nature also implies the arrangement and personality of Wiccan rituals and ceremonies. The core element of Wiccan belief comprises eight seasonal rituals known as Sabbats which are depicted to indicate cycles of life, death, and rebirth, besides seasonal changes. The festivals further allow Wiccans to worship the natural world and align themselves with its rhythm. These Sabbats include the equinoxes, solstices, and agricultural festivals like Samhain, Imbolc, Beltane, and Lammas. Wiccans look for harmony with nature and strengthen themselves with the earth while performing these rituals. Wicca also espouses a significant aspect in its emphasis on gender equality. That manifests in the religion's respect for both the God and the Goddess, reflective of a belief in the equal and balanced nature of masculine and feminine forces. Most such religions value both the divine feminine and masculine as important, compared with many patriarchal religious traditions, and a woman is often the principal figure in Wiccan ritual and leadership. This emphasis on gender equality is quite attractive to many contemporary practitioners, mainly women, who feel oppressed or denigrated within traditional religious establishments.

Many women have found their way to Wicca, which resonates with them as having accepted the Goddess as robust, nourishing, and creative power. The Goddess is regarded in her roles as maiden, mother, and crone. It is commonly associated with the earth, fertility, and cyclical systems of nature. The worship of the feminine is also expressed in magic practice, wherein women are often regarded as powerful spiritual channels. The sacred feminine focus and the doctrine of gender equality in Wicca have made it more appealing to feminists and other seekers who wish to pursue a spiritual path that recognizes equal rights for both men and women. It is from this standpoint that, besides touting gender equality support, Wicca boasts as inclusive and accepting of a whole spectrum of gender identity and sexual orientation. In the Wiccan mind, the balance of opposites, the light and the dark, the masculine and the feminine, takes into account that all are divine expressions, whether male or female, gay or straight. Wiccan rituals often celebrate the diversity of gender expressions and connections, and many proudly openly embrace LGBTQ+ practitioners. A solid foundation for such inclusivity is Wicca's focus on individual sovereignty and respect-for such allows practitioners to manifest their spirituality in forms true to who they are.

Personal responsibility is the other highly important feature of Wiccan ethics. In Wicca, people are believed to have the power to control what happens to them in destiny through their deeds, beliefs, and intentions. The concept of personal empowerment is profoundly connected with the performance of magick, which is actually considered an exercise in focusing one's will to bring change into the world. Wiccans are challenged to assume responsibility for their life, recognizing that choices made affect the situation in which a person finds him or herself and that his or her actions have consequences. A practitioner of personal responsibility learns to trust in the individual self and to discern situations based on a personal moral compass. This equips him or her with a sense of agency and empowerment. Wicca emphasizes the need to maintain a balance between one's own authority and moral responsibility to others. The Wiccan Rede, along with the Threefold Law, remind one that while personal freedom and will are not absolute, they must be exercised in consideration of the welfare of others and in awareness of the interdependence of all living things. They understand the profound impact their actions will have, if one happens to be magic-enchanted or just part of everyday. A characteristic of Wiccan philosophy is that of balance between moral obligation and individual energy, which can help practitioners negotiate trials of modern life in moral integrity as well as benevolence.

Wiccan spiritual philosophy is basically lived. Unlike many other religions, the importance of following a set of beliefs or accepting holy writings as valid, Wicca enables its adherents to nurture their unique experiences with the divine. The Wiccan is encouraged to believe in and to rely upon her own experience and intuition as good sources of spiritual knowing, and rituals, meditation, and magical practice come to serve as a way of realizing direct contact with the divine. Wicca's experiential view of spirituality allows for a wide range of application and experience and represents the flexibility and openness that religion can offer towards individual expression.

Wiccans often describe their spiritual paths as a journey toward growth and learning. Indeed, the practice of magic is sometimes described as a way of strengthening one's sense of self or gaining power and fitting into the natural world. Magic is not about accomplishment or fulfillment but rather a connection and a strengthening of one's tie with the cosmos and introspection. In ritual and spellwork, Wiccans try to enhance their knowledge of their own inner strength, ability to be in tune with the cycles of nature, and with the divine energies that permeate all existence throughout the universe. At the same time, Wicca can overcome those means that oppose its personal growth and transformation. Challenges, therefore, become barriers and trails for spiritual growth and learning opportunities for Wiccans. A Wiccan worldview of life, challenges, and trials is focused on growth as part of the cycle of life but not as retribution or accident. It motivates the practitioner to meet these challenges with self-reflection, a certain level of resiliency, and openness to their mistakes.

Wiccan ethics and philosophy provide a holistic and flexible framework to lead a life attuned to the cycles of life as well as cosmos, balanced within the parameters of nature, and aligned with one's values. In tenets such as the Wiccan Rede, the Threefold Law, and the harmony of opposites, Wicca calls its practitioners to be responsibly, mindful, and compassionate. It also honours the personal freedom, autonomy, and unique spiritual practices of each practitioner. Wicca's open-minded, experiential, and nature-based view of ethics and spirituality has been very popular in contemporary times among all those seeking a means of personal growth, environmental stewardship, and a strong spiritual connection.

CHAPTER II

Core Beliefs and Deities in Wicca

The God and the Goddess

The divine, in Wicca, incidentally, is a duality: the God and the Goddess. It personifies that important balance between masculine and feminine forces. More importantly, this duality encompasses an even broader spectrum of spiritual attributes and qualities that manifest in the life of Wiccan practitioners beyond their being a counterpart to male and female. For the Wiccans, God and Goddess are very balanced yet interrelated forces affecting not just natural cycles but also their spiritual lives. Represented in different forms in the various cultures, they represent very different images; however, they do think of elemental ideas of creation, destruction, and transformation. All aspects as pertaining to God's roles, nature, and meaning, as well as that of the Goddess, need to be known to understand the depth and richness of Wiccan spirituality.

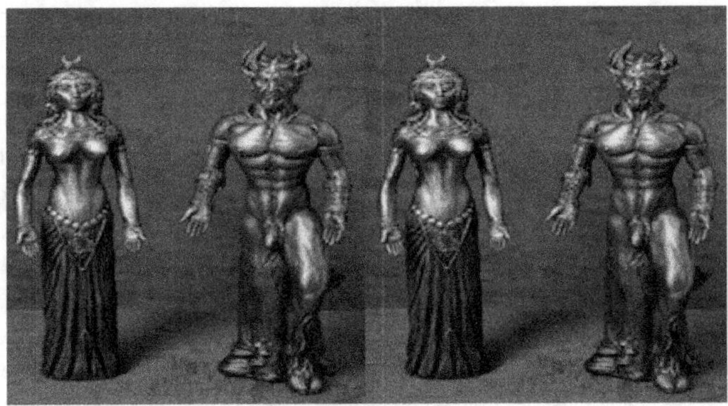

As the principal deity for Wicca, she is often referenced for concepts associated with cyclical life, intuition, fertility, and nurture. She is usually personified with the moon, earth, and natural cycles. Only a few faces will represent the Maiden, the Mother, and the Crone, each representing a different moon phase, each representing a different stage in women's lives. There was the Mother, full of life's sap, fertility, and nurturing, the Maiden, youth, possibility, new beginnings. And the Crone, well, that one represented knowledge, reflection, and understanding that death is part of life. This threefold combination of attributes really emphasizes the rhythmic movement of living and speaks yet more vividly of the value and significance bestowed upon each. There are many other gods of different pantheons or mythoi whom it is said are manifestations of or servants of the Goddess. She may be revered in Wicca under names like Diana, Brigid, Ishtar, or the countless variations of the Great Mother. Since every name has its own mythology and cultural significance, the Wiccans have many pantheons from which they can draw. Nevertheless, if the Goddess comes in another guise, regardless of the form, compassion, empowerment, and closeness with nature will become a uniting thread for her. This is one of the principal reasons Wiccans are renowned for invoking the Goddess in rituals, invoking her wisdom, defense, and inspiration. -the revere of the Goddess for a salutary respect of the feminine divine and also as a counterbalance to much patriarchal influence found in most religious traditions.

God represents concepts of power, action, and protection allied with the male. He's often related to the sun, outside, and the kinetic power of the natural environment. God has all such qualities as bravery, aggressiveness, and an aspiration for development and innovation. Of all his manifestations, he has incarnated the Horned God as the natural cycles and fertility, and the Young God, literally vitality and possibly new beginnings. That is a sign of the Horned God that sometimes is personified by horns or antlers and represents those wild natural characteristics and symbolism for instinct and wildness. This also has concord life and death wherein nature is held due to the sake of all inhabitants on earth. There are also other mythological gods through which God is manifested, just like the Goddess. Sometimes, he is referred to as the Green Man, Cernunnos, and Pan. They represent different aspects of nature and manhood, just as God represents in Wicca's belief. The role that the natural world plays in the Wiccan faith is accordingly symbolized in how God relates to earth and its incidents. Indeed, Wiccans often refer to God in rituals and celebrations in honor of the protective aspects of God and to seek his counsel whenever issues come up. Veneration of the God and the Goddess fosters a holistic view of the deity in which male and female energies are integral to a whole spiritual equilibrium.

Cosmology in Wicca centers its focus on the relationship between God and Goddess, which is meant to be dynamic too and reciprocal. Often, the Great Rite, a holy rite that celebrates their marriage, serves as the symbol for that action. The Great Rite can be performed symbolically within a ritual structure or maybe physical within the structure of a coven; it is much more than sexual, but it is much more symbolic of the merging of energy that characterizes creation, metamorphosis, and in a word, the eternal cycle of life. Wiccan rituals usually focus attention on this marriage as they believe that the balance of energies is to be achieved in order to gain such harmonies of the universe.

This is a long context of the relationship between the God and the Goddess provided by the natural cycles. This basically describes the cycles of life, death, and rebirth through the seasonal changes observed and honored by the Wiccans. The God is mostly worshipped during harvest time and at the end of the year, while the Goddess often stands for the fertile earth abounding in verdant growth during spring and summer. In the cycle of the year, that reminds one of the tides of life when God provides nourishment as well as protection to the earth and the Goddess promises abundance and new life. Because in the way of playing with their energies is a symbol of the inevitable reliance on everything living and of the need of life, in harmony with nature.

One of the key elements of Wicca is the celebration of Wheel of the Year festivals, usually taking place in eight seasonal festivals referred to collectively as Sabbats. Sabbats are the celebrations that mark the cycles of nature and the play of the God and the Goddess. These Sabbats include the solstices, equinoxes, and cross-quarter days. Each must mark a different phase of their relationship and cycles of life. For instance, there's Beltane, a festival of fertility and union of God and Goddess; it falls on May 1 and marks the summit of vigor and expansion. On the other hand, Samhain, at the end of the harvest, is nonetheless a call that the Goddess is leaving and entering the stage of the Crone which would be the process of transformation and death. Each Sabbath reminds one of the eternal dance of God and Goddess in this cyclical rhythm of existence. The deep attraction toward God and Goddess compels Wiccans to question their own perception about gender and divine. It allows a person to come to that place of realized gender, how it really is more of a spectrum than two choices, by presenting both male and female tendencies. By embracing the divine feminine, Wicca inspires its followers to reintegrate their inner sacred feminine, thus subverting patriarchal conceptions of the divine. The religion welcomes the community in just being themselves, outside of traditional cultural constraints placed on gendered identities beyond male/female identification categories. For instance, the God and Goddess can serve as a model for how spirituality, gender, and identity questions might potentially be worked with.

The God and Goddess are archetypes through which the practitioner can find guiding direction along their spiritual paths. Because of their qualities, individuals can relate personally to each god; they speak to diverse facets of the human experience. For example, while a person who needs security and authority would find solace in God, someone who needs nurturing as well as guidance finds solace in the goddess. These archetypes will serve as the very best impulse to call forth more ideas for the practitioner to work with in meditations, rituals, and written reflection. The combination of both gods provides Wiccans with an opportunity to increase their mode of living from a more balanced, harmonious perspective.

In addition to ritual and personal spiritual principles, God and Goddess have moral aspects that nourish the practice of Wicca. The nursing aspects of the Goddess refer to compassion and care for other lives and absolute respect for the earth. She portrays the need to live in harmony with nature and that everything living is connected. The aspects of God in terms of protection refer to power, accountability, and that there is a need to conserve not only the world but its inhabitants. The two form an ethical code guiding the Wiccans to their action towards others, nature, and even themselves. Ethics have been quite well publicized during practice, which is the design for a better way, which has permitted matching the actions performed by the practitioner with the values upheld by the God and Goddess, hence developing accountability and personal responsibility. All of this manifests greater changes in culture and more awareness of the other spiritual views. As an outlook, the God and Goddess themselves have found themselves to change with time because of Wicca's perception. The more that visibility and popularity of the movement grew, Wiccans tended to embrace more diversity in deities and traditions in their practice. Wiccans believe in eclectic theology: they collect representations from other cultural pantheons in search for spiritual paths that hook back to their own, therefore comprehending the divine. In addition to an appreciation for the multiplicity of human experience, many traditions respect those essential principles that unite all spiritual ways.

In this sense of God and Goddess, there has emerged a new recent years recognition in the non-binary and gender fluid identities within the practice of modern Wicca. Therefore, a greater vision for a universal, inclusive spirituality has been promoted with the recognition dawning that the divine does not fit into rigid gender binaries. This means, in other words, the process shown here explains the growth of Wicca as a living tradition that not only meets but also practices requirements by the followers of Wicca. This way, Wiccans can develop lives full of spirituality which can parallel as well as hold up any human experiences and their identity with an expansive view of the divine. In short, God and Goddess stand at the center of Wiccan reflection as well as practice and are expressions of essential harmonies in masculine and feminine opposition. This indicates how all aspects of life interconnect through reflection on the cycle of life, death, and rebirth. This is achieved during the ceremony as well as within daily Wiccan life as people show respect to how those divine energies play through adherence to the Wheel of the Year and cycles of seasons. In this regard, the God/Goddess image invokes fuel for more typical, complex ideas on godhead and makes a person pose questions toward personal conceptions of gender, identity, and spirituality. In addition, the God and Goddess form the very nucleus of a Wiccan life while still being key expressions of power and balance. They force humans to live in harmony with nature; they also lead them through every step of their spiritual journeys.

The Elements and Nature

Elements and the nature world are the bases for the spirituality and practice of Wicca. They believe in the existence of spirit and four classical elements, namely earth, air, fire, and water, where the core powers interplay magic, life, and the intertwined nature of everything. The four have contributed to our vast understanding of the universe and the divine by encapsulating different qualities and symbols. Through the rituals, meditations, and magical practices of Wicca, one respects and works with these elements, thereby fostering deep respect for nature and its inherent energies. This section explores the place of elements and nature within Wiccan spirituality, focusing in particular on how elements shape the practices, ethical frameworks, and structures of belief within the tradition.

Such ideas as elements have originated from ancient Greek and Egyptian thinking, as those consider elements to be part of the universe's vital basis. It is perceived as a concept of old philosophy and metaphysics. In the Wicca tradition, these elements are mainly related to some directions, sea, sons, and qualities. Earth symbolizes materiality, ground, and stability; air is the symbol of thought, inspiration, and communication; fire stands for change, passion, and energy; water symbolizes emotion, intuition, and healing. The spirit that gives life to all creatures in nature and reconnects them to the divine, yet again, is termed quintessence or the fifth element. The earth element has to do with the earthly needs of life and the material world. This is why this aspect plays a big part in Wiccan practice because it symbolizes all these fertility, stability, and nourishment qualities. Earth is most commonly associated with the north side, corresponding with the time of year when winter is in control, which is a season for rest and sleep. They could place stones, earth, plants, or crystals in their altars as a sign of respect for the planet. These factors remind them of the stability and richness that the world embraces.

As Wiccans are filled with a religious belief that the earth is sacred, they regard environmental conservation and life being lived respectfully in terms of sustainable existence. It is within this light regarding their being in interdependence with it, its inhabitants, and its resources that practitioners are called upon to take up their responsibility to care for the world. In reality, most Wiccans have become supportive of ecological activism and are actively engaging in practices that take into account the rights of nature and preserve an ecosystem. This Wiccan ethos, full of respect for life at all its stages and living in harmony with nature, is a clear statement of commitment to Earth. Wiccans generate an awareness of gratitude toward the material world and its bounty by honoring the earth. According to astrology, the air element represents levels of creativity, intellect, and self-expression. It is an expression of the spiritual and intellectual realms of life and also a symbol that reflects imagination, creativity, clarity, and the evoking power of words in feelings. Therefore, spring represents rebirth and growth; thus, its association with the air element and the east. They can tap into the power of the air in Wiccan rituals through the use of feathers, incense, or wind-shaped symbols. These elements remind the person lightly that good communication is highly important and new ideas can take flight.

Breath is fundamental to Wiccans; it connects life with the divine, and breath is one of the most vital connections. Prayer or meditation breathing is the most preferred form of breathing as it allows focus on oneself and consciousness of energies in and around the self. Attention to breath enables a practitioner to be more aware and in touch with the elemental forces. Air is the fact that helps professionals to present their thoughts, ideas, and goals as it encourages a person to express his emotions truthfully and literally in some imaginative way of expression. Fire; passion, energy, transformation. It's linked with summer, when everything's abundant and full of life, and the south. Fire can be a very powerful symbol for spiritual as well as personal change because it sparks creativity and intention to alter. It may honor fire in rituals by the use of candles, bonfires, and lighting up a hearth, as it is symbolic of the light and warmth this brings.

However, though fire has transformative properties, it can both construct and cause destruction at the same time, thus demanding a balance in practice. Witches know that fire symbolizes the throwing away of old customs, beliefs, or hindrances to self-evolution. Transition may equip persons with a lot of catharsis from giving up things that no longer serve them to make space for the new. Apart from inspiring practitioners to act in their lives, fire helps people enjoy their passions and desires. The fourth one is water. It represents emotions, intuition, and healing. Water will signify fall, which accordingly means a time for meditation and contemplation, besides the West. Water is drawn to the studies of inner landscapes and the feelings inside Wiccans because it replicates the fluidity of emotions and the power of intuition. Water can be a bowl, chalice, or other form of a natural source within rituals and remember them by such elements' hygienic and supportive aspects.

Healing with water is strongly embedded in Wiccan rituals. It is believed to have the capability of purifying both the physical and spiritual body. Thus, it is used in many ceremonies for blessing and purification. Wiccans can use the properties of water in their magical practices and, therefore, enhance emotional healing or foster insight and intuition with its energy. Fluidity teaches a good lesson to the practitioner that emotions are normal and part of humans' lives, and they should learn how to adapt and welcome change. Spirit or Essence: That connection, having life force, between physical and spiritual worlds giving vitality in the material world; it is that binding energy between all materials and living things. The spirit is considered to be the inspiration, creativity, and source of connection with the divine. It is to be regarded as being in the center, from which everything appears to converge. A way to build a sort of oneness and interconnection among Wiccans can be the treatment of the spirit to ask for energies that connect and bring together everything.

Being concerned with the spirit as the fifth element motivates Wiccans to explore their path from the spiritual perspective and deepen their love relationship with divinity. Often, this question brings a deeper understanding of one and his place in the universe. The recognition of the spirit reminds Wiccans that they belong to a whole; thus, their acts may create a huge difference in the surroundings. Awareness of this demands accountability towards the actions and well-being of society as a whole. Practices of Wicca are not only theoretical concepts, but also are currently being enacted in practice and ritual, one and all. Each of the elements of which consist of varying relationships of Wiccans with nature and the divine. Invocations of the elements, a characteristic of every sort of ritual, are calling their energies to join in the sacred task that's going to be done. This leads to an energetic interchange between the practitioner and environment, along with the understanding that every one of the elements are living energies, which could be invoked and worked with.

The elements give the witch not only the potential for a connection with nature but also meaningful interaction with it. Each encourages practitioners to tap into the energies that fill their lives and centers magical intent, intention, and meditation. In other words, the earth would seem to center on stability, security, and grounding; the air is called upon for creativity and clarity when working on creative projects; water appeals to healing and intuition; and fire motivates and transforms. The cycles parallel life and the seasons. Wiccans know, like people, that changes occur in human life, as they do on earth- life is growth, decay, and rebirth. In this way, the parts allow the practitioner to make their spiritual activity align with cycles and rhythms in nature. This alignment is always present in Wiccan education to learn how to navigate the movement of flows with their experience and the world around them into harmony and balance. According to Wiccans, the natural world has a great value, not only the elements.

To Wiccans, nature is the sacred expression of the divine; hence, they may be engaged in several practices like gardening and animal husbandry, as well as walks in nature, to strongly feel a connection to the earth. Such respect for nature often sees the value of every living thing, seeing that everything living has a specific role in making up the greater sum of life. Wicca demands the preservation of the environment and natural resources. Above all, Wiccans believe that life is interdependent, and thus, balance and biodiversity in ecology are immensely important. Wiccans are sharply sensitive to the realization that what they do affects earth productivity appreciably. By this realization, followers of this belief system easily find it tenable to encourage sustainable development in society and go about exercising environmentally friendly moves. It also provokes a sense of ownership and stewardship. Many Wiccans are also environmental activists, thereby voicing issues that range from habitat destruction to global warming and the need to preserve the environment. Wiccans want to honor the earth and bring good to it by their actions. Wiccan rituals and celebrations do draw upon the elements and other aspects of the physical world at least to some extent.

The Wheel of the Year is a set of seasonal festivals, which narrate how the elements and the earth's energy are shifting with time. And through each Sabbat, the practitioner is able to honor the cycle nature of existence. Thus, focusing on expansion and fertility at Beltane, for example, coordinates with the fire and earth energies, showing respect to the strength of life. In Lammas, the harvest festival, Wiccans celebrate the abundance of the earth, focusing on earth and water. How nature and elements relate to each other will also help in developing some Wiccan thinking about spiritual and personal growth.

Practitioners are encouraged to find their individual relationship with the elements and understand that no one experiences the elements in the same way. This question often leads to a deeper understanding of oneself and placement within the universe. Take an example of a person attuned to the element of water. They would find they are especially perceptive and intuitive. The eagerness for change and innovation may be possessed by a person attuned to the element of fire. Wiccans come to build a holistic spirituality by connecting with elements and their natural world through interactions with it. This approach recognizes that bringing one's whole self into balance with nature is the only way to achieve one's well-being truly. Some found that being in nature strengthened spiritual bonds for the opportunities for introspection, creativity, and healing. Wiccan spirituality was, to a large extent, based on the natural world and its elements, whether this is done in a group or individually. Further on, the elements can be taken as metaphors for overcoming individual trials.

The elements each have features that practitioners might consider working on themselves to develop or balance in their lives. For example, to seek healing or reflection, a person may call upon the tranquil influence of water for emotional distress. However, to seek inspiration or guidance again, a person who has lost their inspiration or motivation to work towards their interests and objectives can call upon the qualities of fire. In this relationship with nature, Wiccans gain mastery over the events of their lives in a constructive, conscious manner. Being aware of the elements and nature, this concept has thus remained a core in the growth of Wicca. The practitioners added modern thoughts and environmental concerns to their operations and, therefore, increasingly made attempts at trying new ways to relate to these elements. This is a result of the increasing realization of the need to form healthy relationship ties with the earth and the pace through which environmental issues must be addressed. The transcendental quality of all beings also transcends the earthly divisions of species, genders, and identity in current Wicca, which believes that everyone should realize that they rely on each other and have a significant role in the larger plan of life.

As the theme of inclusiveness forms the core of the practice, they are taught that all life interconnects and has its role in the larger design of things. Through this, Wiccans are summoned to dwell in compassion and ethics that enhance the lives of all beings, human and non-human alike, by embracing a broader perspective on nature. The forces within which energies work make reality what it is; the elements and nature, therefore, form very strong symbols of the divine in Wiccan theology and practice. Such elements come as earth, air, fire, water, and spirit, which carry basic ideas about life, thus offering a framework for understanding the universe. The respect for these elements also flows from rituals, festivals, and moral promises towards elements, which therefore allows their deep respect for all the interdependency of creatures.

In a nutshell, Wiccan spirituality is basically and intrinsically rooted in the workings of the natural world and elements that govern all practices, ethical frameworks, and beliefs. The four ancient elements- earth, air, fire, and water- provide a foundation on which everything can find its place; they influence the deeply intertwined web of reality. Wiccans thus walk amidst these elements in rituals, meditations, and festivals, tying themselves in deep reverence for the natural world, and its innate energies. The link to nature and its elements fosters a nourishing relationship with the universe, human development, and ecological responsibility. Change apart, though nothing has changed in the very important place in the religion of nature and elements, which still inspires practitioners to open up to the sanctity of all life and dive deeper into their spiritual journeys.

Other Deities and Spirits

Therefore, the divine, to Wicca, is seen as a tapestry of pluralistic varied deities and spirits founded in many cultures and mythology instead of the God and Goddess. Practitioners could relate to a larger extent of spiritual beings within the model of polytheism that more aptly reflects the characteristics of life nature, and human experiences. Power, another score of extra gods and spirits brought into the Wiccan ritual, also ties one further into the sacred, from which seekers can draw on many sources for empowerment, inspiration, and guidance. This section delves into how a pantheon of deities and spirits interconnects with Wiccan faith and practice so that this tradition is maximally adaptable, inclusive, and spiritually full-bodied.

Many eclectic views on the spirituality of Wiccans would let them accept the spirits and deities of other cultural traditions. This capability to accept others' differences mirrors the knowledge that the divine may appear in different ways to each unique person and their experiences. By this effect, the gods of Celtic, Greek, Roman, Egyptian, African, Native American, and many other cultures could be respected by Wiccans. That diversity is reflected in respect, yet the strangeness of spiritual concepts as being common is also accepted.

Gods depicted in the natural elements and forces, by being known as that which they are or a name by their nature, are the most abstract of all gods representing Wicca. Such gods often fulfill metaphorical purposes in describing some aspects of the natural world-for example, storm energy, phases of the moon, or earth fertility. So, Celtic religion revered Brigid- a goddess of earth's fertility, healing and house goddess. The god Cernunnos, often depicted with antlers, personifies the hunt, wild nature, life and death cycles, etc. Such a pantheon of natural forces reminds people of how they are interrelated and that they must live in harmony with their surroundings.

Lunar gods, often worshipped together with the Goddess, occupy a special position in Wiccan ritual. The phases of the moon cover much of womanhood and life cycles and even intuition. For example, the goddess Selene is often seen being adored as a lunar goddess representing the full moon and transferring the feeling of insight and illumination. Hecate is another great character who has all relation to the crossroads and to the dark moon-speaking transformation, magic, and mystery of the unknown. Lunar deities, therefore, encourage those who practice examining their inner rhythms and intuition more closely and to develop a closer relationship with the practitioner and their spiritual journey. There is also a whole multitude of deities in Wicca's whom Wiccans worship and each of which is associated with their particular theme. Love, war, healing, and knowledge are some examples. To name a few, there is Aphrodite, for example, who is included in rituals about love and romance in general, coming from the Greek mythology culture, representing love, beauty, and desire. On the other hand, the Norse goddess Freyja manifests this duality better about creation and destruction and is associated with love, fertility, and battle. The association of gods and goddesses to the practitioner calls forth specific energies and qualities in ritual and spells, thus enacting spiritual endeavor in a more concentrated, even personalized way.

Wicca allows that, besides the gods and goddesses, there are spirits as well as other beings living within the nature environment. These spirits may be elementals, nature spirits, ancestors, or anything for that matter known to have some influence on peoples' lives or their surroundings. Elements represent the powers of nature itself but are especially commonly attributed to the four elements: air, fire, and water. Other spirits, such as gnomes or earth elementals, have a stabilizing and grounding feel to them. Sylphs or air elementals are thought and inspiration. Salamanders or fire elementals are energy and transformation. Undines or water elementals are the aspect of feeling and intuition. Together, these spirits can help Wiccans improve their magical practice and make a more profound sense of relationships with the natural world. The final important doctrine of Wiccan theology is the concept of ancestor spirits. Truly, to honor and respect one's ancestors, there should be acknowledgment and recognition from those who come after them through showing respect and reverence to their wisdom passed down the years. Many regard their ancestors as guardians and guides who not only help them find their own path but also guide them in the proper path in their spiritual journey. Wiccans build altars to their ancestors and display objects that have a connection to them and their legacy, photos, and other relics. The practice maintains the concept that everyone is a participant in a bigger game of life and creates a sense of oneness and continuity.

In addition to Gods and Spirits, Wicca also utilizes familiar spirits, otherwise known as animal guides. The spirits or guides are, of course, similar to guardians or mentors. These guide spirits are often received through dreams or trance brought on by meditation. They provide practitioners with excellent insight, guidance, and companionship. Familiar is the term used to describe these guide spirits, and it could be an animal figure such as an animal embodying those traits and aspects of the animal. Examples of this include the owl, wisdom, and understanding of the qualities rendered by the owl; another is the fox, that sharp, cunning, and wit. Wiccans can gain deep insight and direction in conducting their mysticism when they attain a perspective or otherwise communicate with their familiar spirits. Since it is an inclusive philosophy, witchcraft encourages practitioners to personally get acquainted with the spirits and deities that manifest in their lives through personal preference and experience. Devotion is an activity through which most people keep themselves engaged in forming a personal relationship with the deities through rituals, prayers, and offerings. It takes on all forms, from praying or reciting invocations to lighting candles and candles and presenting food or flowers. The Wiccans claim that such a presence of beings in their lives enhances the spiritual experience and use those skills as a means of developing a mutual relationship with the gods.

The gods or spirits invoked through Wicca rituals become part of the expression of energy and purpose within the activity being carried out. Rituals may use the invocation of particular gods or spirits to bless a gathering, lead, or enlighten the magic rite that is performed. Such inclusion of others would raise the power of the ritual and, therefore, create a sanctified area where the performer could achieve new forms of contact with the other world. This aspect, as the people celebrate the sacred with one another, gives the participants an opportunity for that feeling of belonging and a common mission. Such a multiplicity of gods and spirits within Wicca further suggests a nod in the direction of encouragement to the tradition towards allowing a person's experience and interpretation. It encourages Wiccans to explore spiritual connections with the supernatural, to find spirits and deities that resonate along their personal path, and thus may provide one with an additional appreciation of their place in the universe and a sense of greater veneration for the many guises of the divine. This way, as they learn and mature in the spirit, even the nature of their relationships with the spirits and gods can change, too.

A tradition of Wiccan divination often seeks answers from the entities in the spirit world, which underlines the importance of other deities and spirits even more. Then there are things like pendulums, tarot cards, and ways of speaking to gods that allow one to get a better idea of the shape of their situation and decisions. Most Wiccans are, in effect, practitioners of divination since they are tapping the energies of specific deities for their assistance as well as to ask for illumination and enlightenment regarding their lives. It thus encapsulates the spirit of keeping open one's ear to the guidance and direction of the spirit world, as well as fostering the very notion of the relationship the gods can instill. It is inclusive towards those creatures in the sense that it reflects an approach showing cultural sensitivity and respect for the traditions from where the spirits and deities are drawn. Practitioners are encouraged to recognize the weight such figures hold in their original context and to worship deities from other cultures with reverence and humility. An understanding of this will only strengthen the belief that every path winds around to the same great universal truths and increase awareness of the diversity of spiritual traditions. This may empower Wiccans to express respect for myriad deities and spirits, which strengthens further the concept of harmony and interdependence among many spiritual traditions.

The third dynamic feature of Wiccan practice, however, is the interface that the God and Goddess have with other deities and spirits. While the God and Goddess sit at the center of the core identity of the religion, other deities and spirits fill out their assignment and make the pantheon richer in character as it presents diversity. This experience gives the practitioner a possible wider horizon of energies and qualities that enhance his expertise. In Wiccan theology, everything shares and balances when all divine beings uphold the source of creation and life. Except for their manifestation of reverence to the gods and spirits, most Wiccans consistently hold rituals that strengthen the bonds of mortals toward the earth and other people surrounding them. Many practitioners regard ground as a living being with its personality, and one has a deep kinship with it. Wicca fosters recognition of the sanctity of the earth and all its flora and fauna by an animistic approach. Interaction between humans and the world and its ecosystems excites the Wiccan to respect the land spirits and try to conserve the environment.

Animism for Wiccans stands for the fact that plants and animals do not only own spirits but differ in terms of their characteristics and wisdom. At some point, a Wiccan feels a need to garner counseling from such spirits so that they understand their knowledge and experience. For instance, the spirit of a rabbit can be represented as fertility and abundance, while that of an oak tree symbolizes power and strength. The practice speaks of the growing respect for life through development and natural consciousness of the surroundings they are living in. The Wiccans and other deities and spirits can also have an element of community bonding because most of them gather in covens to worship the gods jointly. The congregants could invoke the various gods and spirits in such a communal atmosphere and it would result in an identity of shared spiritual cohesion. In this sense, the community unites in pursuit of the holy and challenges each other toward spirituality that will thereafter strengthen ritual and festival potency. Group worship of different gods and spirits gives way to identity and directionality - for which argument one can argue to provide a basis for the fact that spirituality is an activity.

Apart from group rituals, Wicca also advocates for the benefits of individual work and experience. Individual work demands that practitioners reach out to spirits and gods more closely, thus obtaining a more specific expression for their spirituality. This personalistic trend enables Wiccans to be independent and authentic in pursuit since they are empowered to probe into their belief and practices in ways best suited for them. Besides other gods and spirits, Wiccans are also taught to delve into and learn the different mythologies and traditions. Through knowledge about the biographies, characteristics, and natures of various deities, one develops a deeper insight into universal principles underlying the human experience. Such a study encourages Wiccans to look out to outside traditions by cultivating a sense of curiosity and respect for spiritual beliefs as variably varied as they are.

As the practice evolves, so do the deities and spirits pertaining to Wicca. An increasingly aware and encouraged recognition by practitioners of knowing how and in what ways all spiritual practices interrelate motivates them to honor and respect the various cultural origins of deities and spirits that they encounter. This is yet another indication that the sanctity of cultural sensitivity and respect should be brought into the study of the holy. In short words, other gods and spirits found in Wicca make practice richer as well and the relationship between a practitioner and the sacred becomes more strengthened. Thus, given that the Wiccans target a plural but not an exclusionary practice of the spiritual for the worship of many spirits, plus nature and moon deities represent the interdependence of life, the dynamic interplay of God, Goddess, and other divine forces encourages the autonomous and authentic spiritual journeys.

CHAPTER III

Rituals and Sacred Tools

The Importance of Ritual in Wicca

Ritual is extremely used in Wicca because it performs the function of an extremely powerful development tool for the nurturing of a spiritual relationship between the practitioner and the deity, the natural world, and their spiritual self. Other planned rituals are meant to honor certain cycles of nature, or perhaps invoke specific spirits or gods. Ritual is indeed at the center of Wicca for spiritual development, community building, and sacred travel. Rituals are ways in which Wiccans convey the divine to be worshipped, to ask for, and to claim, as well as connected with the earth and its rhythms.

Traditionally, by definition, Wiccan ritual is an act of devotion and adoration. The purposes of rituals are to create a sacred space, or energies, through which practitioners may be in communication with the spirit world. This sacred space is marked by the use of a circle often, in which the circle becomes a symbolic division between the magic and the mundane. It is within this circle that practitioners can achieve an elevated awareness and connect with the energies surrounding them as they're found to be much more focused and comfortable. A sacred space draws people in from distraction and back into commitment and attention, preparing them for the work at hand. Wiccan rituals can vary so much but most typically follow a familiar structure, which can be thought of as invocation, offerings, and performing specific deeds or spells. The structure affords the practitioner the opportunity to convey intention and intent. Through a ritual structure, one draws from established practices that one learns through the years and incorporates the collective wisdom of the tradition. Continuity therefore makes it easy for one to connect with the history of every participant in a larger spiritual history and also strengthens a sense of belonging to a greater Wiccan community.

There are eight feasts making up the wheel of the year which are generally referred to as Sabbats. The Sabbats form one of the most important aspects of Wiccan ritual by which practitioners celebrate the Sabbaths corresponding with the seasonal changes and natural cycles to pay homage to the rhythms of earth and their own. Every Sabbat has unique energies and meanings, so it is possible for the practitioner to concentrate on a theme. It might be fertility and harvest during fall time, which becomes Samhain, or introspection and rebirth with death as the chance to reflect about the ancestors and the life cycle. On the other hand, springtime Beltane is all set apart for fertility and growth themes. The Wheel of the Year rituals give the practitioners a way of harmonizing one's experiences into the natural world. Wiccans, through their yearly rituals, come close to embracing their bond with the land and the cycles that feed all life. This harmony urges the practitioners to live in harmony with nature and fosters appreciation for the treasures of nature. It reminds every one of the need for ecological consciousness and stewardship over the earth where people are more and more separated from nature.

Other than seasonal festivals, Wiccan rituals are conducted for different purposes like healing, protection, or manifestation of desires. The implementations, symbols, and correspondences are used in the rituals to satisfy the specific purposes for which the practitioner conducts them. For example, a healing ritual would include certain incantations to healing deities or goddesses, crystals associated with wellbeing, and medications that have been identified to have restoring properties. Customizing a ritual which answers one's intentions is quite essential in amplifying the intensity and concentration of one's energy. This allows practitioners to actually potentiate the effectiveness of their magical workings. Rituals can empower people by giving them a sense of action and agency. Rituals give individuals a meaningful way of controlling their lives and experiences. In a society where a great part of its members is often consumed with either the crippling feeling of powerlessness or detachment from the environment, agency assumes special meaning. Rituals provide practitioners with a means to give expression to their will and thereby actualize their aims, a way in which they may reassert control over their lives. In the formation and practice of rituals, it is intended to preserve the idea that human beings can be masters of their own destiny as well as the destiny of the rest of the world.

Other aspects of rituals in Wicca are aimed at solidifying relationships with the adherents through extension of community attachment. Group rituals among the adherents, mostly conducted in covens or during meetings at community events, make the members feel more united and purposeful. A group ritual can create communal energy that has the potential to be profoundly transforming in amplifying the work that is being done. The members will support each other in hard times and share successful moments to accompany one another on their spiritual path. Wiccans heavily depend on the element of community as a constant reminder that they are not traveling this journey alone. Wiccan rituals also facilitate strengthening relationships within a coven and hold reflection and personal growth opportunities. Individuals are led through their inner landscapes, their fears, and their passions in the ritual setting. Wicca uniquely emphasizes the reflective aspect of the ritual because it enables the practitioner to access a sense of verisimilitude, or truthfulness, about himself. Add quiet time, meditation, or even writing in a journal as the most common rituals that link the person to their inner self and perhaps illumination of one's spiritual journey. Self-discovery is an extremely important process for growth and helps in finding ways in which one makes his or her actions meet goals and ideals. In this case, the effectiveness of Wiccan rituals would need to be highly centered on the symbolism attached to them. Symbols are specific meanings and energies that may heighten the ritual experience. They can be colors, elements, or instruments. For instance, green can be very responsive to rituals focusing on abundance because it is usually positively associated with growth and reproduction. The same holds for the elements: earth, air, fire, and water-itself the fundamental forces of nature, so they can give the ritual its very own special quality. Symbols and correspondences are drawn closer to the energies by the practitioners and further and deeper for a more intimate experience.

Ritual has the very important function of honoring the divine through God and Goddess, but other deities or spirits. It is in their invocations and gifts that ritualists develop a bridge connecting them with the divine by calling these spirits into the hallowed realm. This connection elicits a sense of wonder and appreciation within the practitioner because it returns him to his rightful position in the cosmos. Wiccans reaffirm their commitment to their spiritual paths by publicly declaring their beliefs and values in a ritual recognition of the divine. Lunar rituals: Wiccan rituals reflect the cyclic nature of the universe and life. As the seasons and the moon are diverse, so are people's lives. Rituals enable people to give meaning to their lives as well as add meaning because they serve as channels of transition about those experiences. Human beings can relate the rites with aspects of the life journey that they can be noting the pain as a result of the loss or indeed excitement as one embarks on anew. These teachings also prepare practitioners to be fiercely and flexible-minded because they will learn to hold onto the highest peaks and lowest valleys of their lives.

There is formal ritual in Wicca; nonetheless, ritual can also become something that filters into everyday life. Much of a practitioner's every day can become ritual-filled with daily rituals that inject intent and awareness into sometimes mundane events. For instance, an effective ritual for invoking spiritual consciousness could be to affirm something every day, light a candle while meditating, or even thank for the meal. Ritual brings in the concept of presence and a relatedness that gives Wiccans the space to discover the sacrosanct from the mundane. The other proof that a ritual offers scope for creating the link of continuity and tradition is another importance of it in Wicca. Wiccans often speak about "ancient customs, traditions, and teachings passed down through the ages." This heritage of knowledge supports a belief in an existing tradition, and it will make them feel that they belong to and are connected with the larger Wiccan congregation. In some sense, Wiccans can bridge the distance between their experience and the amassing of wisdom in the tradition by being respectful of old customs.

Apart from the continuity of existing rituals, practitioners are challenged to be innovative and make new rituals. The creative element of ritual-making allows people to express their spiritual identities and personal values. Whether that is creating something new from nothing or innovating a pre-existing model- for example, practitioners may inscribe their personal goals, experiences, and insights into whatever work they undertake. That is such an innovative process that allows the individual to feel any control over spiritual practices that are given unto them and empowers them to undertake acts positively on their spiritual journeys. Rituals are also very effective channels of transformation and healing. One of the most common practices that Wiccans use regards emotional scaring, trauma, and personal struggles. Many therapeutic rituals employ affirmation, visualization, and the use of either crystal or healing herbs. Conscious participation in the ritual process might well provide a safe environment for healing and reflection that enables practitioners to work through things they have experienced and move toward wholeness. It is this transformational nature of ritual, that the special stress falls on Wiccan practice as being therapeutic in the sense of affording humans a means of kindly and intelligently traveling their inner terrain.

Added to Wiccan rituals it is possible to build up a sense of purpose and meaningfulness. In rituals by setting intent, people are reminded to think about their intent, principles, and desires. This focus on intention-setting pushes people toward putting their behavior into line with their aims, which, in turn, creates a feeling of being in control and moving forward. The expressed intentions within the ritual context are then made more meaningful; they are interpreted as a promise for the purposes of materializing those intentions. Stronger to this thought, the procedure would be to facilitate actual working in and for the goals of the practitioner so that they understand the fact that yes, indeed they are psychically able to consciously create the realities that they experience. The social nature of rituals shall also provide an avenue of common experience and group intention. Group rituals would enable participants to come onto a common vision by themes of unity, cooperation and mutual assistance. This sense of community can be especially important points of major life transition, marriage and birth. Gathered together to share these momentous times, practitioners deepen their bonds with one another and form a network of love and support. The shared group experience of ritual underscores the importance of connection and cooperation to Wiccan practice.

Wiccan rituals may be personal and collective meanings, but they become acts of worship for the planet and living on it. Many practitioners admit that there is a sacredness to nature and include aspects of the care of the environment within their rituals. This ecological awareness is evidenced in festivals representing seasonal changes, when practitioners pay homage to earth's cycles and fruits of its plenty. By realizing the interconnectedness of everything living, Wiccans may be able to build a sense of better environmentalism that will allow them to work toward ecological sustainability. Ritual plays an important role in Wicca, which matures in the modern era. More and more practitioners are learning about the critical role rituals play regarding the issues and complexities of modern life. This can be in the form of new themes, traditions, or emblems that define the contemporary culture. The Wiccan can be assured of their spirituality not being one behind in time by only having its rituals updated to suit the life in the contemporary world.

In a nutshell, ritual plays a great role in Wiccan practice because it helps one to connect themselves to God, nature, and the self. Thus, the ritual can clearly demarcate its intention, honor the cycles of life, and foster a sense of community and individual development through the very structuredness of its process. More than ceremonial proceedings, rituals are important because they run through everyday life to give even mundane events their spiritual context. Wiccans may walk the path of their spiritual experience with awareness and vision, and in deep respect for the interconnectivity of all that is, by accepting a power of transformation within the rite. Counterexample: Wicca-a powerful connection it has to the life of a practitioner carried over in the rite, where practice makes it easier to locate the holy in a world that deeply finds itself in flux, and this rite's enduring significance.

The Sacred Tools of Wicca

Sacred instruments hold a very important place in Wicca. They strengthen the relationship between the practitioner and the divine, so they facilitate the manifestation of intention. Therefore, these objects are at the same time imbued with personal meaning and hold a role as a visible entity and a symbol for the forces, elements, and gods Wiccans worship. Every object has a special role and meaning to such an extent that its application in the ritual is instilled with beliefs, goals, and the particular energies he wants to invoke. The text encompasses numerous sacred equipment Wicca uses, their applications, spiritual associations, and importance. The athame is a ceremonial dagger used to direct energies. This is one of the most important tools in a Wiccan ritual. Double-edged and sometimes a symbol of passion, will, and change, the athame is often associated with fire as its element. While most associate it with being a cutting and carving tool, the biggest function of an athame is to help focus energy on spellwork and rituals. In reality, the athame blade represents the active and passive elements of creation; therefore, it symbolizes the existence of conciliation between both masculine and feminine energies in Wiccan practice. To those who cast protective circles, call upon gods, or even use it as a means of directing their energies in spells, the athame can be a great tool. In a rite, holding the athame helps to energize the practitioner to let him feel that he is more connected with the forces he uses and his desires.

The chalice or cup is one of the most important Wiccan items that symbolize the divine feminine as well as the water element. A chalice is a container that is primarily used in the reception and keeping of sacred liquids such as herbal infusions, wine, and water. The chalice is used, then, in rituals for blessings, offerings, and feasting. It is an access for the practitioner to honor fertility cycles and cycles of life. That part of the inner psyche and the fluidic aspect of life is attracted toward the chalice. Abundance intuitions, and emotional depth are implied. It is when he drinks the contents in the cup that act binds him to nature and in the patterns of life by symbolically partaking in what is best in the divine and earth. This is another important tool that is a very significant icon in the practice of Wicca, often attuned with the spirit as well as that of the element of air. Generally, wands are far more organic and made of wood materials and also used in the invocation of a deity, in the direction of energy, and in circles. A practitioner can focus their desires on the universe with the wand as an extension of their will. Just like people, every wand is unique, and practitioners generally personalize them by choosing certain kinds of wood, crystals, or symbols that are close to their person. That closeness enhances the power of the wand because these practitioners embed their energy and intentions into it. The wands can establish contact between the spiritual and material worlds and, in a broader sense, between the divine and occult elements of the natural world.

Wiccans usually combine the said major instruments with huge lists of additional sacred objects to aid their practices. A pentacle is one of the most meaningful protection and harmony symbols as a five-pointed star enclosed in a circle, which symbolizes earth. The pentacle is made from clay, metal, or wood to convey the spirit and the four elements: air, fire, and water. The pentacle is a powerful symbol often used in rituals and spellwork; it also makes an excellent centerpiece for altars and as a tool for energetic grounding. The pentacle's circular shape reminds one of a connection with all living things and life patterns. It is also the symbolism of unity and completeness. Another artifact that is used almost routinely in Wicca is the bell. This cleanses an environment or is rung to mark when a ritual is beginning or ending. The ringing bell converges with the spiritual energy in it, but it absorbs good energies and fights bad ones. It tells the practitioners to focus on their intention for the sacred ritual by reminding them to be present and attentive. The ringing of the bell by the practitioners demarcates space as a place of magic and intent, and the sonic barriers are, in themselves, avenues that enhance the sacredness within that space. This tool specifically defines the role of the auditory aspect in a relationship with the divine and the importance afforded to sound and vibrations in terms of spiritual practice.

This is also very important in Wiccan traditions, for they each have special energies and qualities that can improve spellwork, rituals, and personal development. Often, crystals are chosen for an association with some aspect of the goal or healing properties. For example, rose quartz with compassion and love, and amethyst for its calming and protective qualities. The Wiccan uses crystals to enhance the intent and energies of a ceremony; he will place them on altars or carry them about with his person. This organic vibration from these stones constantly reminds the user of the strength of the soil and of the innate charm of the natural world. Wiccans thereby strengthen their relationships with the surrounding energies and elements. Another very popular tool used in Wicca rituals is a candle, which symbolizes fire, as well as the divine spark of life. There are various colors of candles-they are assumed to represent different kinds of energies, purposes, and gods. For example, a green candle might mean growth and prosperity, while black candles are often used as a sign of protection or the eviction of negativity. Lighting a candle in the ritual helps guide the intent of the practitioner as well as light up the sacred place. The candles symbolize the power of regeneration of potential and changing energy and signify the transformative powers of fire. This is a powerful beacon of inspiration and optimism, making practitioners tap into their inner light and divine destiny via a flickering flame.

The most crucial element of Wiccan practice is the altar, a form of sacred space for the performance of rituals and gods worship. Typically, many holy objects, symbols, and offerings describe the intention and belief behind the altar adorning the intention and belief of the practitioner. Altar objects can include things such as candles, crystals, incense, goddess representations, or mementos that have particular significance to the practitioner. While an altar allows people to prepare and maintain a sacred space in their home, it emphasizes the relation that exists not just to the surroundings but beyond it. In that sense, as an altar acts as a locus of reflection, acts of meditation or mere religious practice can converge to underscore that the sacred and the mundane exist in harmony with each other. Incense is one thing that a lot of people use during their Wiccan rituals for the purpose of purifying a space and drawing divine presence to a ritual. Certain kinds of incense are used for certain energies and intentions, such as meditation with sandalwood, protection with frankincense, or calming with lavender. The ritual ambiance also carries the sensory effect produced by incense burning, which challenges participants to involve their senses in this spiritual activity. Incense burning when the sweet smoke upsells to meet the sky, giving the participant's desires to the heavens, is an offering. This practice is used in Wiccan rites to emphasize the role of scent and other sensory characteristics in the rituals, furthering the point of interdependence of the material and spiritual realms.

In Wiccan rites, deities also play an important role through symbols and images. Statues, representations, or symbols of God and Goddess, as well as other gods and spirits, can be added to altars and rituals. Generally, the images of these depictions usually draw the sacred into participating within the sanctified space as the means of becoming the initial points of the acts of adoration and communication. For example, they might find a closer relationship with these gods and goddesses through various offerings and petitions to gain guidance, inspiration, and, sometimes, aid. These symbols do allow the practitioner to explore mystical ideas and occurrences in that they deepen the practitioner's relationship with the divine. Tools are very personal objects except for their functionality. In order to infuse their tools with purpose and power, most practitioners take the time to bless and consecrate them. Often, they have rituals for the elements, gods, and energies involved with each item as a part of this process. Practice needs practitioners to sanctify a connection between themselves and their tools by consecrating those tools for purposes, making the functionality of the object used in rituals and spellwork. With the close relationship, ordinary things become sacred objects in Wicca practices, and practitioners find empowerment in their craft.

Sacred tools hold meaning more than for practical use alone; they represent the path and the intentions of the practitioner. This is what enables all of them to become spiritual, evolve or change, and connect with divinity. With the conscious practice of these rites, the practitioner will be led to an understanding of her desires, her needs, and the desired forces. The exploration and process of self-discovery form the basis of the Wiccan path that encourages people to accept their diversity in spiritual pathways.

Sacred tools are an exciting yet-to-be-developed part of Wicca's heritage as it matures. Modern practitioners need only craft their own or craft antique tools according to their own practices and ideas. This evolution enables Wicca to be perceived to reflect all the implications of expressions and, therefore, put greater emphasis on the value of personal interpretation and creativity in spiritual action. Practice flexibility allows Wiccans to try out new instruments, symbols, and methods that best speak to their real lives. By using sacred instruments, Wiccan practitioners can express their spirituality since these instruments allow them to utilize their creativity and intuition. Most Wiccans enjoy crafting their instruments themselves, whether it be to prepare concoction herbs for rituals, hand-carve a wand, or configure a personal altar. This creative process allows practitioners the freedom to be expressive by using the tools, and it is this that leads them to a deeper sense of ownership over the spirituality they practice. Sometimes, the preparation of the sacred equipment can be a very fulfilling and life-changing moment that justifies the basis of spirituality being an activity in flux.

They could, therefore, be termed sacred tools representing part of the spirituality and the practice that involves the activities of Wicca. The athame and chalice, wand, pentacle, and incense, among others, all bring about their own meaning and use to allow such practitioners to connect with the divine, the natural world, and also the inner self. This meaning gives rituals, tightens bonds within the coven, and demands personal growth. This rite refers to flexibility and the concept of its application in the Wicca practice which gives rise to the justification for sacred tools. Wiccans can be able to delve into their belief, spiritually grow, and walk their paths with intent and authenticity if such tools are hallowed and utilized appropriately. Sacred tools of Wicca call forth the wonder and beauty of life by reminding them that material and spiritual worlds are interwoven.

The Altar and Sacred Space

While altar and sacred space are used commonly in spells and rituals as well as in personal spiritual practices, they play a significant part in Wicca. An altar is more than just a physical structure-an altar becomes a space set apart by the practitioner to honor nature and communicate with the divine to channel their aspirations. On the other hand, the holy space refers to the area of use meant for spiritual exercise; they are mainly characterized by a sense of security, concentration, and heightened consciousness. Wiccan ritual worships at the altar and the holy space that gives room for meaningful connecting with the spirituality and energies surrounding.

The altar will eventually be the core of the Wiccan ritual and celebrations. It can be something as plain as an altar table decorated with artifacts that may symbolize something or as complex as a specially designed building integrating with natural material. A design for an altar often reveals the views, goals, and tastes of the specific practitioner. Common things one finds on an altar include candles, crystals, goddess representations, herbs, incense, and mementos special to the practitioner. Every object on the altar has its purpose and, altogether, they help carry the energy and intent of the room. One of the most personal and transformative acts a practitioner can make is building and maintaining an altar. It is rare for practitioners to spend hours not even days selecting objects that evoke a sense of meaning and symbolism for the altar. This brings natural introspection and contemplation and now a renewed sense of connection with the tools and rituals of your craft. The altar is a context in which this person will place their own will and desire into this sacred space. Building an altar is, in fact, the real physical expression of a Wiccan belief and intent because it quite often symbolizes the path.

As the central point of energy and intention, the altar is often placed at the center of Wiccan rituals. For one, this circle becomes a borderline between a place entirely sacred and the outer world, which the practitioners oftentimes cast during the ritual by circling around the altar. It acts as a protection boundary that allows the practitioners to work freely with energies and spirits without interruptions by the outer world. Being the focal point of such a sacred plane, the altar is only a conduit for the energies being sought, thus aiding in intensifying the spell. The altar is considered a place of reverence for the divine or Gods and Goddesses. Many Wiccans like to have statues, pictures, or symbols on their altars as a form of representation of these deities. The images put on the altar enable the gods to enter into rituals, and consequently, the unity relationship is established with the spiritual world. After being reminded of one's place in a larger universe, this devotional act also serves to perform the task of preserving the magnificence of the role of the divine in practice for Wiccan.

The altar is associated with the four elements-earth, air, fire, and water-and expands on the meaning. On each of the elements on the altar, commonly represented by specific items or symbols can be found in these elements. An example would be, plants or crystals for earth, incense or feathers for air, candles for fire, and a chalice or bowl of water in replacement for water. With these elemental symbols set up, the practitioner establishes harmonious balance in one's holy space, and one understands how everything adds up to a total. It is within these rituals that participants can tap into the alignment to the elements, which opens access to natural energies at play during the ritual and, in turn, raises the power of the altar in general. Part of the idea of sacrosanct space is the context through which a practitioner might arrive at approaching their spirituality, something greater than the altar in its literal sense. The act of designating an inside or outside space in order to focus on doing spiritual activities is creation of the sacred space. Often this place, where energy, intention, and reverence are congruent, has assisted practitioners in being taken to another plane of awareness. Preparation rituals for a sacred place include purification rituals such as smudging with herbs or sprinkling sea water to purify the surroundings and attract positive energy.

There is a safety within holy space to allow being able to enter here so the person will be able to focus on the spiritual task and nothing that will distract will actually be in the space. In such a setting it allows to be mindful, and, therefore, people are more connected with their intentions and with the energy they are working with. It acts as a vehicle for the exercise of spirituality in this regard and offers practitioners a comfortable and nurturing environment in which to examine their conceptions and aspirations critically. It must be balanced how pivotal the role of ritual is in the creation of sacred space. By invoking the various spirits and gods associated with such a type of holy place, ritual can transform a prosaic space into the magical or meaningful place. It is this ritual consecration of space through which practitioners carve out a definite connection between the natural and supernatural worlds. Often using sacred objects, mantras and offerings in this work, it amplifies the energy of the room and invokes higher spiritual beings.

Many would have their sacred space mark the moon phases and the natural cycles of the seasons. Some may want an altar outdoors during the full moon because that would be used to tap more positively into the lunar cycle. Tuned in to nature, it reminds them of the ebbs and flows of existence and thus strengthens bonds with life cycles. It is appreciation of what nature offers that makes practices that honor the earth's rhythms and serves to make people understand all forms of life are intimately connected. For Wicca, personalization is very integral to the altar as well as sacred space. In fact, it is often averred that one must charge the spaces with his energies and intentions so that the environment can speak for his particular spiritual path. One can personalize one's object through especially meaningful colors, symbols, or even components. Practitioners can build a personal space through which they can ask questions authentically about their spirituality by making it according to their beliefs.

The altar and the sacred space interact; each will evolve through one's lived experiences, as well as from personal growth. The altars of people may change and look different as they walk their spiritual journey, filling in with new understandings, concerns, or goals. That flexibility allows a practice to be living and thriving, specifically suited to each practitioner's needs and goals. It is this fluidity that enables them to pay respect to the dynamic nature of their spirituality and the transformative power of ritual. Sacred space and the altar are also needed for those Wiccan rites that focus on community building. In group rituals, often participants will convene in a holy space and give their energy and intentions over to the work of the ritual. Therefore, the communality of holy space illuminates and energizes the rite, a firm underpinning support for groups' intention-setting and spiritual inquiry. Group process in the act of creating and then relating to a sacred space develops bonding between practitioners, increased unity and shared identity among those bonding.

Personal altars open opportunities for other practitioners besides the group ritual work; people share their designs, practices, and inspirations much. Inspiration by them sparks creativity and friendship in them; it challenges practitioners to try new ways of spiritual activity. Since the altars are individualized, Wicca presents different kinds of manifestations of different pathways each person takes. Practicing the altar and sacred space develops mindfulness and presence in daily situations of life. Most practitioners often find a bit of time to admire the divine and good things that would exist inside and outside and the ways through meditation and thanksgiving rituals that would be happening with the altar. Purposeful concentration on gratitude helps practitioners become aware and appreciate the beauty of existence while building connection with the present. Wiccans cultivate an inclusive manner of living, sacred and mundane alike, with mindfulness evident in their spirituality.

An altar and sacred space are the ideals of Wicca, the community of Wiccan people, and the reality of the individual practitioner. A holy place is established and used with respect for the natural world, divine, and interdependence in life. Living according to such principles brings a kind of spirituality that honors Earth and all its habitants under the canopy of Wiccan traditions. Therefore, in this busy and increasingly discon185ned world, the holy space and altar serve as reference points for contemporary practitioners. The conscious act of choosing a place for action amidst spiritual activity imbues one with purpose and grounding from which one can get on with current challenges with aware intent. There is a grounding quality, making the holy spaces and altar seem more ritual- and practice-focused on the fostering of spiritual exploration and growth.

Because the history of Wicca is so readable in the altar and sacred space, it remembers even as it changes and evolves to meet any given situation. Gradually but surely, practitioners start coming to realize that there must be settings constructed which respect personal experiences amidst collective communal sense. According to Wicca tradition, this awareness brings a resilient and flexible environment with the capacity to adapt to change, yet to hold fast to spiritual roots.

All this to say that the altar and holy space are relevant parts of Wiccan practice as they ensure the connection to the divine, the world of nature, and to oneself. With the altar as an object of attention, ritualists can voice their intentions and show respect for the sacred. Sacred spaces can be considered areas of safety and respect inviting reflection and spiritual growth. For Wiccans, these spaces cultivate a closer sense of kinship with their community, the natural environment, and their own spirituality. The altar and holy area encourage those using the space to participate in an unfolding, dynamic practice, honoring the interdependence of all life and one's journey. As Wicca adapts and flourishes in the modern world, the altar and holy space remain a vibrant emblem of the power and determination of the tradition: a means by which the practitioner can touch the sacred in an unfolding world.

CHAPTER IV

Wiccan Holidays and Wheel of Year

The Eight Sabbats

The Wheel of the Year represents the cycle calendar by which Wiccans honor cycles of the seasons and cycles of nature. Its most important elements are the Eight Sabbats. Each of these marks an important date in the agricultural calendar as well as some particular astronomical occurrence, such as a solstice or equinox. Wiccans pay homage to god, the natural world, and to life itself as connected with these festivals. The Eight Sabbaths are not only jubilant celebrations and times for contemplation but also a time under which spirituality and transformation are being tested.

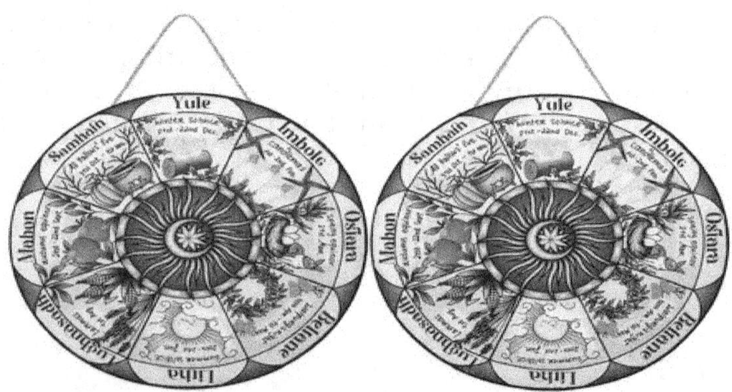

Samhain is October 31st. This Sabbat introduces winter. It is, as well, the end of the harvest season. In a way, Samhain is the Wiccan New Year, because it reminds folks to remember their ancestors and think about cycles of life. They believe that this is the time when one may call up spirits as well as the dead, because this is the thinnest part of the veil between two worlds. Wiccans construct altars with offerings to the ancestors and light candles to make a path for guiding spirits back home. Traditional food items shared that represent an abundant harvest are apples and nuts. Samhain inspires draisines to reflect on the pleasures of life and its woes by making use of this reminder as an expression of the cyclical cycle of life. Yule, Winter Solstice is on approximately Dec 21. It comes right after Samhain. Yule is the longest night of the year, time of rebirth and return of light. This Sabbat celebrates the God reborn at this time and is often represented as the Sun. Traditionally, Wiccans celebrate by decorating Yule trees, burning candles, and exchanging gifts. The Yule log, usually burned on the hearth for protection and comfort, is an ancient tradition. Participants in this celebration of light returning to Earth are invigorated to reflect on personal inner light and the possibility of rebirth. The process of making New Year resolutions is an act of hope and a new beginning in life. Yule, therefore, presents practitioners with a perfect reason to make resolutions concerning the new year.

Imbolc occurs either on February 1st or 2nd. This sabbat is anticipated to be a celebration of the transitioning process of winter to spring. On this day, Goddess Brigid is celebrated; she embodies inspiration, healing, and fertility. Traditional candlelight used for Imbolc encompasses candles lit as a thank you to Brigid, but also signifies the return of the light. Practitioners are allowed to use rushes or other kinds of natural material with which to produce the traditional Brigid's crosses which bless and protect them. With all of the energies and vibrations that surround this springtime season, it would remind people of the deed to create and inspire as well as to act on goals and objectives. Ostara is observed around the time of March 21st-the spring equinox when night and day were of equal length. This Sabbat honors the Goddess in her virgin aspect and celebrates the balance of light and dark. Ostara, or spring equinox, is hinted at by blossoming flowers and waking earth, and thus stands as a time for fertility, growth, and rebirth. Indeed, many Wiccans celebrate this rebirth of life into the soil with decorated eggs, sown seeds, and one hundred thousand crafts. Perhaps one of the symbols, that of the egg, is a particularly powerful symbol of possibility and new beginnings. Ostara challenges the practitioner to think on what they want and the actions that will bring this into being, as well as embracing change and growth in their own lives.

May 1st is Beltane. This Sabbat marks the end of spring and the beginning of summer. It is a festival praising the God and Goddess together, and a colorful acknowledgment of sexuality and desire and fertility. It is ritualistic in action. One such practice is the dancing around the Maypole. It represents both masculine and feminine energies in their union. According to Beltane rituals, bonfires need to be lit to signify fertility, protection, and purification. Practitioners will also leap or dance over the fire to call in blessings for growth and abundance. Beltane encourages merry appreciation of the small pleasures of life and the creative energies that uplift and inspire. It is a time to generate happiness, excitement and relationship building and enabling one to express desires. The time in the year when there is the longest day of the year is June 21st, coincidentally Litha, a celebration that takes place close to this date. This Sabbat honors the earth at its peak power and full strength and riches while it honours the Sun at its zenith. As much warmth and light, the sun brings into the lives of the practitioners, Litha is alive with joy, thanksgiving, and awareness of being with nature. Traditional rites and rituals usually involve gathering herbs, flowers, and other natural materials for spells and blessings. Many Witches light bonfires on the night of Litha to acknowledge the power of the Sun and to celebrate how its energies must just grow on. Litha invites a spirit of respect for the natural world and all that it provides when reminding to cherish one's gifts from the earth.

Lammas, also known as Lughnasadh, marks the beginning of harvest season on August 1st. Abundance and the first fruits of the earth are sab batted at this time. This may be the most usual rite associated with Lammas, though is that of baking bread as an offering to the gods- an activity frequently calendrically tied into gathering grains, especially wheat. Many Wiccans celebrate this time by hosting group feasts to thank for what they have harvested. It is also a time to honor to remind a community of its value and of how all things interdepend. In Lammas, practices are encouraged to take stock of their harvests, monetary as well as spiritual, and how one might distribute one's bounty to others. The Mabon is the last Sabbat of the Wheel of the Year; it falls on or around September 21-the day that falls on the Autumn Equinox. Now that the seasons are levelled, that long day, short night, this Sabbat is also time to celebrate. It's a time for introspection, and giving thanks to go into harvest, to prepare for winter, and how to spread the good fortune throughout the Wiccan community by potluck in the recognition of an abundance throughout the world. One ritualistic act is making a cornucopia full of seasonal fruits and vegetables to symbolize harvest plentifulness. It encourages practitioners to reflect on the past year, think about what they have done and what they have failed at, and then make decisions for the coming months. It helps people understand the importance of harmony and balance and incites them to foster appreciation and consciousness in everyday living.

In the support of each of these Eight Sabbats can be a way of engagement by the Wiccan with the cycles of nature and the divine to make a journey all the more profound. The Sabbats encourage every person to participate in customs and rituals thriving on respect towards their environment, celebrating community, and offering scope for development and growth for the individual. The cyclical nature of the Sabbats; it gives the impression that life is a journey that would never come to an end, in that every season will bring a new opportunity to learn and grow. Watching the Eight Sabbaths also arouses feelings of kinship among the practitioners. So vast in numbers are the Wiccans who go to these, strengthening links of support and friendship. The rituals are performed among groups, thus providing a space for the sharing of blessings, intentions, and experiences all of which heighten the concept that spirituality is often an activity encompassed by groups. This feeling of community is highly essential for individuals in this fast-paced world in which most people believe they have lost touch with nature and their spiritual selves. The Sabbats are anchors, by which people can pause in the midst of the bustle of daily life.

The eight sabbats can also be used as a template for reflection and goal setting. Each festival requires a practitioner to consider his development, objectives, and goals. As the seasons shift, there is a natural cycle during which time it's nice to reflect on life and goals. There is always room to reflect often. This cycle model trains the people to take positive steps in meeting their aims while appreciating the natural surrounding environment. Moreover, this process helps people feel more responsible and goal-oriented. But Sabbats offer still more space than introspection alone: creativity. Herbs in sachets, ritual implements, seasonal decorations-all this and much more can be found incorporated into the celebrations of many practitioners. Through these applied practices, practitioners incorporate their spirituality into creative pursuits which bring joy and meaningful engagement with the world as it is. By itself, the act of making becomes, then, an act of devotion, pouring purpose and meaning into all its products.

Stewardship and ecological awareness The Eight Sabbats emphasize so much stewardship and ecological awareness. Being a part of natural cycles and seasons means Wiccans grow in their own understanding of the environment and all living things in interdependence. Many initiates practice rituals with a focus on sustainability, conservation of the environment, and social service by acknowledging the reality that the initiates are health care providers on the planet for posterity. Modern Wicca is much concerned with ecological awareness, which is the expression of raised awareness about the need to share life in rhythm with nature . The eight Sabbats remain as part of the Wicca tradition as it evolves. How this has been expressed in the past is often adapted by modern practitioners for their times. Their versatility continues to invest Sabbats with relevance and weight because it allows people to connect with the cycles of the natural world in ways that resonate within their own experiences. The new themes, symbols, and rituals are only testimony to the fluidity of Wicca and promote the significance of personal interpretation and creativity.

The Eight Sabbaths, for their part, urge one to delve deeper into the mystery of life, death, and rebirth, rather than just being some good days to celebrate. Every Sabbath encourages one to reflect on the placement of where they sit in the larger universe-a closer affinity with the divine, the order of life and another. It shows them more consciousness of the cycles happening in their individual lives by embracing the Wheel of the Year as a cyclical passage that inspires personal growth, transformation, and healing. All this comes together in the Eight Sabbats, which are an integrated part of Wiccans' rituals, giving them the framework to mark the change of the seasons and to respect everything that is alive in its own interrelated nature. Every Sabbath therefore presents unique opportunities for reflection, community and creativity that invite practitioners to connect with rhythms of nature and spirit. This remains part of Wicca's heritage to date, as this rite reminds practitioners to become a little better acquainted with themselves in regard to their spirituality and place within the world. Wiccans celebrate the glory and messiness of the journey through life, and that is reflected in the fullness of existence by celebrating the eight Sabbats.

The Esbats and Lunar Worship

The holiness of the moon and the Esbats comprise all features of Wiccan rite that spice up the seasonal Sabbath celebrations. "Esbats are gatherings around the full moon, new moon, and other phases of the moon, offering practitioners the chance to reverence the lunar cycle and engage themselves in rituals, magic, and social events with other practitioners.". Many spiritual traditions used the moon as a symbol that represented passion, intuition, and the tide of life. Wicca lunar worship extensively relates to earth's natural cycles. This makes it possible for the practitioner to be in tune with both the natural and cosmic cycles.

Moon worship traces its antecedents back to the old cultures when the moon was considered god or a powerful celestial force. Many prehistoric farming societies knew how the lunar forces affect tides, plant growth cycles, and fertility cycles. Thus, life-and-death cycles and soil fertility often were associated with lunar deities. The moon is often represented as the Goddess in Wicca: it stands for fertile forces of Nature and feminine spiritual power. Through this connection to the Goddess, one can attune himself with his emotional perception and build much deeper intuitive sensitivity-not to mention find his feminine energies.

Esbats are usually performed at night, under the full moon. As it is very bright during this time, it is said that it is in the most powerful and most enlightened state of the moon. As this is believed to be often a rather lifting energy, the rituals, spellwork, and manifestations are best performed during such a time. The practitioners come to pay respect to the moon and to thank it for lighting up and guiding them. Some of the rituals done during a full moon Esbat include divination, circle casting, and god and spell evocation; these include protection abundance prosperity. While the full moon esbats center on completion and fulfillment - letting go of things that no longer have a place in your life and embracing new beginnings - new moon represents potential and darkness, fresh starts and personal growth. The new moon is the first day of any month, and its ceremony focuses on planning and sowing seeds for the future month. Some of the other rituals that would be suitable for this stage might include journaling or silent reflection and goal setting. This is a time when they can make a vision board or write down their intentions to see what they intend to bring into their lives. By focusing on intention-setting, people can voice their wishes with regard to lunar cycle energy and thereby achieve the dreams in question.

The moon has phases, and each of the phases has special energies and opportunities for magical activity. Wiccans celebrate not only the new and full moons but also the waxing and waning phases of the moon. That period between the new and full moons is the time of the waxing moon-time for growth, attraction, increase. Rituals for attracting love, money, and new opportunities in life shall be one of the center points for this phase. Such people who wish to have something in their life, just for the sake of evolution may light up candles or do charms and spells. The moon waning, which follows after the full moon, is for letting go, banishing, and release. The practitioner is instructed to think of whatever in his life does not seem to be in service anymore and acts towards its removal.

Such a process of releasing might be very liberating because it can enable people to overcome fears and limitations and clear some spaces for new growth and opportunities to sprout.

Additionally, it urges moon followers to develop a more intimate relationship with their inner guidance and intuition. The moon phases can be used as a checklist for processing emotions and self-discovery or inward reflection. One common Wiccan practice is keeping a lunar journal in which one writes down his or her feelings, ideas, and experiences about each phase of the moon. Since practitioners believe that their emotions are real and relevant, they get energized to become more mindful of their emotional landscape. If attuned to the moon's energy, people's spiritual path can become enlarged and they get a deeper sense of themselves. One important thing about the Esbats is that lunar worship merges the religious practice with the surroundings. In fact, many persons performing the esbats would prefer ceremonies outside because it would be partly a gesture of respect for nature and the way moonlight permeates all surrounding space. This rite can inspire a kind of cosmic awe and respect in human beings through observations of how the moon changes in all its phases. Gathering of natural material for magical work, such as spellwork and offerings in flowers, stones, and herbs, is part of the ritual elements. This contact with nature forms the basis of the conviction about the role of the moon, understood as a dimension of earth's cycles and rhythms rather than as an independent entity.

Many Wiccans also work with quarter moons, where the moon falls at both the first and last quarters of the lunar cycle besides full and new moons. The First Quarter Moon Encourages Practice In this regard, the full moon acts as a period for action and resolution. It can be in form of promising to do something, undertaking a project, or acting heroically. For example, the last quarter moon forces them to check themselves and get rid of all things one needs not to have. It is a reflection and letting go of things.

The rituals of Esbat play an important part in Esbat life because it serves as an opportunity for the practice to connect with each other, share stories, and encourage one another in such spiritual journeys. Group rituals can bond together and guide the power of rituals. In fact, many Wiccans claim that attending Esbats inspires them to belong more to the community members. Support as well as belonging among the others are encouraged by these events. The practitioners are allowed to discuss their experiences, methods, and thoughts on moon worship and magic at these events, making knowledge flow. In reality, Esbats could be something of a formal ritual or something of a more casual get together. Some practitioners will prefer to do it alone where one prepares their lunar worship space suited to their individual practices and traditions. Others will participate in a larger group rituals where everyone celebrates the moon and all it has come to represent, and feasts, games, and songs are the common celebrations that have been shared. The basic goal hasn't changed, although the festivities must now be adapted: pay respect to the lunar cycles, then connect to the Divine and meaningful spiritual practice.

Moon worship and esbats necessarily evolve with Wicca as modern practitioners develop their desires and preferences. For most Wiccans, aspects of folk magic, in addition to regional tradition, are incorporated into their Esbat rituals-they borrow from these sources. Because of this flexibility, Wicca allows the practitioners to add unique ideas and experiences to their rituals while adhering to the dynamic nature of the practice. Lunar worship is based on the same principles, only the values now refer more specifically toward respecting the cycles of nature and a closer relationship with the divine and with oneself. Except in some ritualistic congregations, the moon has significant meaning for Wiccans. Frequently, it is believed to inspire and guide one through a more practical day-to-day life. Followers may utilize these cycles of the moon to keep attuned to their emotions, goals, and intents. People living according to the lunar cycle will sow harmony and balance within themselves and see life as formed from many cycles, changes, and transitions. Knowledge itself talks to people about change; for knowledge only makes a person stronger and more supple.

The Wiccan concept also well corresponds to this lunar mythos as a metaphor of the divine feminine. For many practitioners, the moon represents the Goddess, while the qualities that should be linked with those are wisdom, nurturing, and intuition. Connection in life encourages people to honor different expressions of who they are and to find their own femininity irrespective of gender. Forcing people to have extremely high self-awareness of one's spiritual journey, lunar worship makes them receive their creativity, intuition, and emotional depth. Lunar worship is bolstered by the fact that many different cultural traditions associate the moon with various gods and archetypes. The Goddess is commonly represented in Wiccan rituals as wise, good, and strong in her moon aspect. In their Esbats, practitioners may invoke certain moon deities, such as Selene, Luna, or Artemis, in hopes of receiving advice and inspiration from these celestial intelligences. Furthermore, by situating moon worship in the context of even larger myth, the practitioner reap for themselves all of the knowing and stories of countless traditions, all the richer for practice.

Lunar worship within part of Wicca involves instruments and symbols connected with the moon as well as rituals both individual and group. Objects that can be employed to reinforce this connection and invigorate the energy of the rituals include silver candles, selenite or moonstone crystals and all sorts of images of the lunar cycles. Moon water, or charged under the moon, is also produced by practitioners and is utilized in spells, rituals and purification practices. It makes use of material from things, a function which pushes the users to practice their spirituality in other dimensions, a point that propels this concept of spiritual and physical being integrated worlds. It also appreciates the presence and awareness. To ensure an environment of reverence and sensitivity of nature, the practitioners take breaks to behold and respect the moon and the phases. Besides the ritual congregation, this consciousness has already started monitoring phases of the moon by the rest of the crowd and self-reflection concerning one's emotional state and goals as they perform their daily activities. Even glancing up at the moon is enough to remind the students that the universe is vast and that they are just a small phenomenon in it, thereby sending and installing resonance and unity.

Wiccans still draw inspiration, healing, and empowerment by the continued practice of lunar worship and Esbats. The respect for the moon and cycles serves to bring practitioners closer to their emotions, intuition, and spiritual routes. With communities availing themselves of the use of the Esbat rites, meditations, and gatherings, personal growth and change are prompted by the encouragement of people to find the mysteries of life, that of themselves, and the divine.

In summary, the Esbats are part of Wiccan practice, with moon worship and veneration feature; thus, there are opportunities for reflection, friendship, and spiritual growth. The climax of the Esbat celebrates the cycles of nature, God, and the divine feminine by remembering all phases of the moon and makes it a more profound sensibility that connects with emotional wellbeing and intuition. As an adaptable sequence of rituals, lunar worship gives people room for creativity and personalization in their practices, which makes lunar worship relevant and useful in actual practice. To embrace the stories and energies of the moon, the Wiccans would take their unique stories and immerge them into the rich tapestry that is lunar worship to achieve an increased awareness of who they are and where they stand in the universe. That is, at its deepest, Esbats calls practitioners into meaningful and transformatively engaged encounter with the holy, with nature, and with one another-through reminding them of the beauty and complexity of reality.

Celebrating the Sabbats and Esbats

Underpinning the spiritual life in Wiccan practice are the Sabbats and Esbats, which are those festivals that give rhythm and structure to the practitioner's path. There are two complementary yet distinct aspects of Wiccan spirituality in these: the Sabbats, marking the eight seasonal festivals of the Wheel of the Year, and the Esbats, which celebrate the phases of the moon. Together, they foster the spiritual development of the individual as well as connection with the environment and universe. Being knowledgeable of the manner in which the ritual should be conducted will strengthen one's relationship with the divine, earth, and the Wiccan tradition. The Wheel of the Year is a yearly cycle derived from patterns of seasons and cycles in the agricultural cycles.

This cycle consists of the eight Sabbats, of which some are extremely important turning points and comprise the following: Samhain, Yule, Imbolc, Ostara, Beltane, Litha, Lammas, and Mabon. Every Sabbath has its own conventions, themes, and rituals that find a place in every traditional and contemporary culture. Although reverence for the cycles of earth and consideration of their own lives within the natural rhythms makes a space to reflect, the change that can see itself is able to observe the Wiccan New Year, known as the Festival of Samhain, celebrated on October 31st. This is a reflective time and honor those gone before because when the harvest season nears a close, it is drawing winter in. Since this is conceived of as the tenuous veil that separates the realms, the rituals assume candle-lighting and setting up altars in honor of spirits to welcome the dead. Practitioners may create a sacred space that venerates life and death; they can do a reading to attain knowledge or speak about their ancestors. Samhain challenges people attending this event to examine what took place during the past year and how they will do better in the year ahead. Yule falls approximately around December 21st, Winter Solstice. It is after Samhain.

At this time of the year, this Sabbat celebrates the return of the Sun and the regaining light. Some of the most current activities that take place during Yule are decorating Yule trees, lighting candles, and giving as symbols of rebirth and hope. The log is that which has historically been burned in the hearth for it symbolizes protection and warmth during cold winters. The Thanksgiving idea can be interpreted in several ways, including going over the good things that happened the previous year and attempting to make resolutions of what they might do differently in the coming year. Yule is a very apt reminder of cycles of life, resilience, and rejuvenation. Imbolc falls on the dates February 1st or 2nd, marking the transition from winter to spring. It is commemorated by paying reverence to the goddess Brigid, who actually represents inspiration, healing, and fertility. The rituals are quite many; rush crosses and candle burning to be an act of worship before Brigid and returning light. To tap into the power of inspiration, participants can also creatively participate in poetry writing or handicrafts. Those who observance this will tap their inner creativity and prepare for spring growth. Ostara falls on or around March 21st-the; day and night are equal to the Spring Equinox.

This Sabbat depicts the waking of nature and celebrates fertility and balance. Activities include planting seeds, decorating eggs, and checking the resurgence of life on the earth. Ostara is the celebration of a new beginning, and it holds its value through taking action to get what one strives for. People reflect on things they'd like to do over the months ahead and see which things they would like to bring into their lives. The rebirth and fertility themes empower the person to be tolerant of change and growth. May 1st falls under Beltane, which is the final day of spring and the first day of summer. This Sabbat celebrates the union of the God and the Goddess; it is a joyful time full of fertility, sensuality, and passion. In such rituals during that time of year, there are rituals of fertility rites, lighting bonfires, and dancing around the Maypole. The practitioners would enjoy such an event to pass good times with love and affection for the little happiness of life. The second situation would let more liberality in expression and a traced behavior in people with real passion and impulse for creativity. This magnificent celebration of life evokes deep respect for the simplicity of beauty in life. Litha Lithuania falls on or about June 21st. It is the time to celebrate appreciation for the year's longest day. It is also known as the Summer Solstice.

It is also a celebratory day of energy and fertility because the Sun is included in its rising. Some of the rituals are picking wildflowers, herbs, etc., and beginning bonfires to symbolize the Sun's force. Practitioners acknowledge that equilibrium must exist for them and that they thank the earth for everything it offers. Litha challenges people to celebrate their successes and reflect on their desires before they sow their passions.

Lammas begins the harvest season. It is August 1. Many of the common celebrations of first fruits have roots and involve baking bread to share a feast. This is a time for practitioners to reflect on their own harvests, material and spiritual, and give thanks for the abundance they have received. Lammas festival challenges a person to know how life is connected and remember to importance of community and sharing. This festival challenges the practitioner to regard their own development and think about how they can better other people's lives. Mabon is the final Sabbat of the Wheel of the Year, falling on or around September 21st-that was also the date for the Autumn Equinox.

Time of balance this Sabbat means because day and night are now equal. Mabon is a harvest festival of thanksgiving. It calls on practitioners to take stock of the last year, to realize what they have, and to be thankful for it all. One of the ritual practices is to make a cornucopia with seasonal fruits and vegetables inside as symbolizing an abundant harvest. Mabon gets people to thank, engender community feeling, and go in for the cold winter. Wiccan practice is not limited to only Sabbats; it includes the Esbats-lunar cycle days also. The rituals to honor the moon power and enhance more magical operations are performed during full and new moons in most of the Esbats. The full moon is always associated with high energy, so it should be fully used for spiritual activity, divination, and manifestation. In worshiping the light of the moon, priests and priestesses meet to perform their rituals, which may include casting circles, invoking deities, and spells under protection, abundance, and intuition. In Full Moon esbats, one receives the completion and fulfillment requested; therefore, it is a letting go of whatever no longer serves oneself and opening the door to new possibilities. This is contrasted in the new moon, which symbolizes rejuvenation and renewal and time for darkness and possibility.

Some common rituals related to the new moon include goal setting and intentions. Practitioners can create vision boards or write down their intentions for the coming month, which means what they want to bring into their lives. The new moon inspires people to set a plan and introspect and align objectives with the intent of the lunar cycle. In practice, as they form their goals, this exercise provides a feeling of power. More importantly, these cycles of waxing and waning provide clear avenues for magical work.

A waxing moon phase is the period between the new moon and the full moon. This is where growth, attraction and expansion happens. Spells in the waxing cycle can center on attracting new potentialities and good energies into a person's life. The waning moon is related to letting go, getting rid of and deposing. Soon after introspecting what is no longer serving them, practitioners act to remove obstructions and negative energy. This cyclical perspective of life, providing a sense of mastery and nudging them to be the author of their spiritual journey, means celebrating the Sabbats and Esbats can really create a profound interdependence with the divine as well as nature. One of the common behaviors by which Wiccans celebrate is spending time outdoors with other natural companions for this puts them in close proximity with the cycles of the earth. When they observe the way the moon changes, and then they can see how the seasons change, it fills them with wonder and reverence for the cosmos. The most common rituals involved gathering natural materials for conducting spells and offerings such as flowers, stones, and herbs. This makes it even stronger that earth and cosmos are interconnected just because we relate to the natural world. The connection of the Sabbats and Esbats must also be a bond for the practitioners in their communities because it helps them associate with each other, share stories, and sometimes interact with each other.

Group rituals further nourish the ties of brotherhood and sisterhood and merge into the ceremony in a more vibrant way. As these festivals encourage bonding in the community and mutual support, many Wiccans have discovered communion with lots of benefits. Indeed, the discussions of spiritual journeys and related practices, ideas, and experiences make these gatherings knowledge-sharing events also. Esbats and Sabbats may be marked in the most formal of ceremonies, and in some cases, mark it in casual gatherings. It could be their means of showing it, preparing ritual spaces which are specific to the practice and belief. Other people join in more elaborate communal celebrations, like feasts, games, and singing. Always at the root of the practices is Sabbats or Esbats: for the purpose of observing the rhythms of nature, entering into contact with something greater than the self, and undertaking meaningful spiritual practice. Of course, the Sabbats and Esbats also offer ways to recognize the importance of awareness and mindfulness.

A practitioner will learn about, come to respect and even appreciate the natural world by taking time to observe these astronomical events. More than the old pattern of gathering, this mindfulness encourages the person to pay attention to the moving and settling seasons and moon cycles, and to listen to one's own feelings and needs as the ordinary world rushes by. It would even become a very easy reminder for the practitioners of the space of the universe and may evoke the feeling of connection. The Sabbats and the Esbats evolve as the practice of Wicca develops in order to include respect for the needs and preferences of the practitioners living in contemporary society. Many ideas that will inspire their own celebrations Wiccans will find in folk magic and regional customs. Flexibility is dynamic nature of Wicca allowing practitioner's to add their own thoughts and experiences into rituals. Their core aspects - things, namely, the significance of offering respect to cycles of nature and developing closeness to God and to oneself-don't change with time. Beyond the rituals, the Sabbats and Esbats serve greater meaning in Wicca.

They charge initiates to accept the change and transformation on the self as a real revelation of the life, death, and rebirth process. Every ritual calls for a realization that life is just an in-flux movement all along. Living contact with the Wheel of the Year and the phase of the moon becomes a catalyst in intensifying the balance and harmony and the connections realized in mundane worlds. In a nutshell, Sabbats and Esbats observance forms the backbone of the Wiccan tradition as it is the platform for development of relationship with God and nature. These seasons introduce individualism, community, and awareness about life cycles. In the process of observance of mysteries of the Sabbats and Esbats, meaning and belonging can be developed through rituals, pondering, and experience. For that matter, such celebrations are wonderful reminders of how rich and complex life is-to connect with the divine, the world, and others in transcendent ways. The Wiccans appropriate the richness of life by placing themselves in tune with the moon and the rhythms of the year.

CHAPTER V

Wiccan Practices and Magic

The Role of Magic in Wicca

Magic, in Wicca, is essentially transforming and basic as it connects the material and the spiritual. Instead of how one gets what one wants, Wicca views magic as a deep understanding of energy, purpose, and the interconnectedness of all things. Wiccans try to harmonize with nature cycles in the cosmos by materializing the purposes they want using the powers of nature, elements, and the divine, thus making use of magic for spiritual and personal development. To understand how magic works within religion of Wicca, one has to review the origins, uses, moral implications, and meaning of it for the individual.

Essentially, Wiccan magic is based on the basic assumption that all that lives and is a part of nature is interconnected, and energy flows throughout the universe totally. That view basically draws upon deep, longstanding spiritual practices and traditions that underpin the importance of both intent and the natural world.

Concentrating the will and intent, Wiccans believe they can influence the energies around them in order to create effects they desire in their lives. This popularly is referred to as "spellwork," an overarching term that encompasses the wide spectrum of practices, ceremonies, and practices that harness magical energy. Wicca usually performs magic through the use of objects and symbols as places of energy and purpose. Everyday magical instruments include symbols, crystals, candles, and plants; each symbol embodies some kind of energy or quality. Candles of various colors can be employed to symbolize different objectives, such as using green for prosperity, pink for love, and blue for healing. For instance, plants have been attested to possess various mystical energies. For instance, flowers, herbs, and grasses have been connected to love drawing, purification, and protection. Crystals, on the other hand, are used by practitioners for their energetic value; the suitable type of stone is sometimes sought after to derive specific intent in spells.

According to Wiccans, a boundary is created between magic and the world through the establishment of sacred space as a precondition to any magical act. This space is often created by casting a circle as it will hold the energies raised in the ritual and protect the practitioner from extraneous influences. The circle is a symbol of totality, unity, and the cyclical aspect of life. Invoking the elements, God and Goddess, and other spiritual entities within this space allows practitioners to create an amenable space for their magical operations. Spellwork often involves a deliberate process that could include such steps as prep, intent setting and energy building. As such the base of any spell, the practitioner begins by stating what he or she wants to attain concisely. A defined goal is crucial since it directs the magnetic energy to an intended result. After establishing the purpose, practitioners gather all the necessary tools and materials and go through several rituals that build energy. To this end, a Wiccan might chant, dance, visualize, and apply other techniques to focus and intensify the energy within the circle. Finally, the spell is cast into space, where it is hoped that the right energies combine to create the desired effect.

Since it is assumed that Wicca practitioners will approach their spellwork with respect and responsibility, ethical questions regarding magic are very relevant. Many Wiccans follow a philosophy guided by the Wiccan Rede, which is "An it harm none, do what ye will." This philosophy emphasizes reflecting on the consequences one's actions may have for oneself and others. Wiccans believe in the Law of Threefold Return, whereby every energy put into the cosmos is returned to its source. That way, it gives the magicians a motivation to do good, constructive magic that furthers balance, harmony, and well-being to all. Wiccans use magic for the benefit of others and the greater community, not for themselves. Practitioners of magic are often healing magicians, offering their talents to friends, relatives, or even complete strangers in need. This "working for others" attitude promotes sympathy and a sense of oneness, which in turn provides impetus to believe that magic is curative and restorative.

There are also Wiccan groups performing rituals based on collective intention, such as the spells for peace, prosperity, or environmental healing, which immediately emphasizes the collective character of magic. Wicca also employs magic, beyond being useful, as an excellent source of self-actualization and self-discovery. Spells allow practitioners to face their fears, pursue their passions, and understand the journey of the spirit. Generating and guiding energy Wiccans gain insight into what they aim for, as well as what drives them, and cultivate a feeling of autonomy and accountability in life. Self-discovery often leads to wonderful personal growth because it teaches people how to navigate their inner landscapes and live according to their values and beliefs.

Wiccan practice can further use the positive, creative and inspiring potential of magic. Many practicing witches view spellwork as an artistic expression, creating unique rituals and spells that touch base with their own experiences and beliefs through their imagination and intuition. By use of creativity one can, in such a way add his or her energy and standpoint to one's magical practices in order to create very crucial and highly personal rituals. The ability to make and perform magic can then also be seen in itself as a way of meditation while amidst the agitation of ordinary life. It speaks of an oasis for reflection and mindfulness. Self-discovery is one of the important emphases within Wicca, along with the important bonding of magic with the cycle of the seasons in nature. Most practitioners comprehend that spellwork is highly coupled with timing, and in practice, they tend to align their works with the moon phases and the Sabbats. For example, one is believed to attract or create new chances and opportunities with the waxing moon but will banish and let go on the waning moon. Practitioners can continue bonding with the earth and strengthening their magic by working in rhythm with these cycles.

Also, Wicca's view of magic as cyclical matches more general themes in life, death, and rebirth. So many spells and rituals concern transformation, acknowledging change is not something to be feared but rather embraced in embracing new beginnings. The above view promotes flexibility and elasticity, challenging the practitioners to perceive blockages as means of growth and development as well as learning. Wiccans approach their practices with modesty and openness, realizing that practicing magic is much about dancing in an infinite cycle of life rather than being about achievement in the world of things. Magic in modern Wicca is transforming, inspired from various spiritual paths, cultural experiences, and individual pursuits. It is common for many practitioners to borrow, combine, and interpret folk magic, herbalism, and other forms of esoteric tradition in order to weave a profound tapestry of magical techniques that reflect their personal perspectives. Versatility and adaptability are characteristic of Wiccan magic, permitting practitioners to experiment with and to try out different methods, devices, and ideas. As such, Wiccan magic is an ongoing, living art forever changing to meet the needs and demands of its practitioners.

Magic also comes into play in Wicca through strengthening a feeling of belonging and community. There are usually group rituals and meetings in Wiccan traditions that allow the practitioners to bond and merge to a shared purpose and celebration. These may generate a better climactic energy than regular rituals and do inspire a sense of unity and purpose. Practitioners forge close friendships and a support network of others who mutually uplift each other in their spiritual journey through shared experience. Such a sense of community lends a much deeper understanding to the idea that magic is a group experience which could transcend both space and time, rather than being solely an individual practice. This role of magic has stayed intriguing and mysterious as Wicca continues to pop up on the charts in modern popular culture. It has managed to capture the interest of people who wish to rediscover old customs, delve into spirituality, and establish a tie with the nature world. This renewed interest in magic and spirituality is best exemplified in the long-term popularity of Wiccan concepts. There is an increasing interest in holistic, natural activities, and this trend reflects an even broader cultural movement toward the acquisition of health and well-being. Practitioners will be able to share information, experiences, and ideas with others, which will give depth to the function of magic in Wiccan spirituality.

Briefly, magic is multilayered in Wicca: it encompasses a broad spectrum of actions and intentions as well as the calculation of ethical regard. Magic is a way of entraining one's will to the cosmic energy. It is self-discovery, personal empowerment, and rapport with nature through the transcendental process that, in discipline, spade work insinuates ideas, beliefs, and intentions. Their ethical basis, in accountability and empathy, lend the argument a support for the belief that magic should be used for the good of society in general. Wicca sees magic ultimately as doing with regard to the great tapestry of creation, personal growth, community and in a way closer than previous religions allowed, to the divine, rather than about trying to achieve specific objectives. They embrace the beauty of spiritual path and life, death, and rebirth within themselves when they celebrate magic.

Spellwork and Types of Magic

Such applications of magical principles for accomplishing something are milestones on the spiritual path for a Wiccan. Interaction with energies from the universe boosts the will of the practitioners to impact change within their life and also outside in the world. The spellwork, therefore, is a multiverse process involving a variety of techniques, tools, and approaches due to the different nature of the numerous beliefs and practices of Wiccanism. By knowing all the different kinds of magic and subtleties of casting, practitioners may explore more advanced stages within their craft to become ever the more proficient in how they manifest their desires in a manner acceptable to one's moral compass, as well as acceptable to the seasons of life.

In essence, spell working is based on the premise of the nature of everything having energy and that it is possible for human beings to come into a connection with that energy to make what they desire happen. Because

Wiccans are believed to possess vibrational frequencies, they believe that all the energies in the universe communicate through one's thoughts, intentions, and emotions. Therefore, intent and manifestation involve the most crucial part of magic practice because it teaches the practitioner on how to direct his will in affecting the flow of energy in a manner that favors his objectives. Wiccans are instrumental agents in their lives through the process of creating and transformation using spellwork . Any process involving spellwork always starts with the intention of a clear objective. This is because the direction of a spell would always depend on a clear goal. The Wiccans have enough time to think about the reasons behind any actions they wish to bring into their lives thus making their goals based upon moral values as well as ethical principles. A clear intention also acts as a focused intention to bring clearly into being the practitioner's energies. The intention is the heart of the spell; this serves to channel the practitioner's energies toward a focused result, be it protection, healing, prosperity, or love.

Following purpose, practitioners will gather all their materials and tools that will help spellwork. Wicca has long used candles, crystals, herbs, and symbols as magical tools. Qualities are unique to each tool, and these will attune to the uses and energies in one or multiple ways. Candles of different colors can be selected; red candles can represent passion and love, and green is often used for claiming to have a claim to wealth and abundance. Herbs are also quite important in spellwork; many practitioners utilize the magical quality that a plant possesses to enhance their rituals. For example, rosemary is prepared with the intention of doing protection and clarity while lavender is mostly used to do relaxation and cleansing. Spellwork is the act that follows preparation, energy raising, and release; one of the most common acts in preparation for spellwork involves drawing a circle, which is preparing a sacred space or the drawing of the circle, separating the magical from the mundane. The circle keeps the energy generated during the ritual. Worker can easily concentrate on his goal and objectives without being distracted by anything outside of that. Workers can invoke aspects, Gods and Goddesses, or any other aspect of spiritual being to create the type of environment that will be needed in the space for magical activity to happen.

Energy raising refers to the process of gathering and condensing the power needed to fulfill the intention. It is during energy raising that the spellwork becomes crucial in fulfilling the objective. For purposes of energy raising, one may use techniques such as drumming, dancing, chanting, or even visualization techniques. It is through these techniques that human beings can energize and vitalize their intentions in a bid to connect with the rich energies of the universe. The process thus becomes highly individualized by tapping into the subject's own rhythms and modes of spiritual communication through energy raising. It has to be released into the universe after the energy has been generated. It cuts the energy to the intention and releases it so that maybe in the world it can materialize. The practice is often set with the image of one's intention appearing and feeling all the emotions that come with its presentation. This release moment is important only in serving to represent that act of letting go and faith that the universe will bring the intention about through energetic alignment. At the end of the spell, then, the practitioner can ground themselves and thank the gods and forces which were called upon during the ritual before returning to the material realm. As if magic could take so many forms, it would be useful to keep aware of the varied ways Wiccans might practice it.

One of the most common practices of magic is sympathetic magic, based upon the concept of like attracts like. One of the most widely used tools in doing sympathetic magic is using images or symbols related to that which is desired. For example, if he or she is looking to bring love into his or her life, he or she would make a doll or poppet that represented what was the perfect mate for him or her to be. The energies would then be directed toward attracting love into his or her life by focusing their intention on the representation. There is elemental magic, another important type, which used and tapped the power of the four classical elements: earth, air, fire, and water. Because each of them has its special properties and connotations, an individual has access to the energies associated with his/her use for making spellwork enhanced. Earth is particularly favored with protection or prosperity spells because it stabilizes, creates abundance, and grounds everything. Inspiration or clarity-based spells draw power from Air who represents reason, thought, and inspiration. A potent representative of passion, change, and psychic ability, the use of Fire provides for high usability in spells that call for bravery or inspiration. Lastly, water is said to represent emotions, instinct, and cure and thus offers scope for practitioners to come up with spells that would work well in emotional cleansing or well-being. Practitioners weave a complex web of energies while calling on the elements to empower their spells and strengthen their desires. There is healing magic, another practice of Wiccan; this is helping practitioners control their energies to make them beneficial both to others and oneself.

Rituals, prayers or visions meant for mental, emotional, and spiritual healing are often enacted within this kind of magic. Herbs, crystals, and many more healing aids can be used by the Wiccans to emphasize their intentions of helping the suffering person regain his or her harmony and balance. Healing magic is based on holistic health because it has to do with an acknowledgment of the interconnection that there is of the body, the mind, and the spirit. Protection magic is also something that most

Wiccans learn. Such magic has for its intent the prevention or blocking of any evil influence, energy, or intent that might jeopardize peace or wellbeing. Workers may use a number of techniques including casting protection charms, setting up safe areas if they cast circles, or using some plants or stones which are thought to possess protection powers. Protective magic is that power infuses in people, which makes them secure and confident at every walk of life. Divination is the absolutely fascinating and intricate form of magic that may take the forms of divination, where individuals are seeking the spiritual world for intelligence and insight.

Pendulums, scrying mirrors, tarot cards, runes, and many more tools Wiccans use to probe their intuition and heavenly guidance. Apart from revealing the secrets of the future, divination is a very potent practice for self-reflection and personal transformation. Divination teaches the practitioner to look inward for motivations, fears, and desires and increases the strength to align one's goals with spiritual ways. Another type of spellwork that Wiccans perform is candle magic, which involves the symbolic meaning of candles. Because every colored candle has its own energy and intention, practitioners can then pinpoint just what their spell needs. Light the candle in a ritual, anoint it with oils, carve inscriptions or symbols into the wax-many candles in spellwork include these elements. Practitioners view their intentions being released into the universe as the candle burns, allowing the energies to flow in the direction of their wants. Another fascinating aspect of Wiccan magic is known as kitchen magic.

The tradition compounds on a feeling that mundane tasks such as cooking food or any activity that is invented in the home can be turned into magic by focusing attention onto the energies that are involved with the food and how it is being prepared. They can prepare recipes consistent with their aims, bless their food or even use a few plants or ingredients for their magical intention. The kitchen magic always holds the sacredness of food and powerfully weaves spirituality together with family and food. Lately, very often met the green magic that highlights reliance on plants, natural materials, and earthly energies in magic making. Such magic requires close contact with nature and realization of its wisdom and might. Herbalism, gardening, and foraging can all be part of a Wiccan's activities-that can bring energies into spells and rituals from the source itself: plants. Green magic connects the practitioner to the energies diffused through all living things and natural cycles. It has also been associated with sustainable living, consciousness and care for nature. With every advancement of the Wiccan practices, technology is ever more integrated into spellwork and may be added.

Some research their magical work based on online data, applications, and other digital resources. This new aspect of spellwork has made it more accessible and easier to interact. Thus, even more people may share information and insights, as well as mutually exchange encouragement within virtual networks. On the face of things, there does appear to be a contest between technology and tradition; however, in many ways, Wiccans have learned to synthesize both well; they realize that it is actually the connection and intention behind the magic that matters little what form it takes. Spellwork is one more significant feature in the practice of Wicca, and it comes under the rubric of an ethical imperative that happens to be utterly crucial. This is what the Wiccan Rede reminds participants in spellwork, not to harm another. It presents a time for reflection on what goals one might want and to think of the repercussions that it would do to someone or something. This teaches responsibility in the use of magic with respect to creating energy for more good than bad and that the energies produced do not clash with well-intentioned positive intent. A well compassionate and mindful practitioner has a closer connection with the universe and their art when casting spells. At first glance, spellwork is quite a diverse and colorful feature of Wiccan practice, which, also contains a very wide range of methods and implements, and magical kinds.

Practicing spellwork enables practitioners the ability to seize the power held within the universe so they may venture further down their spiritual journey to touch nature and manifest their desires. The scope of such a type of magic, whether it falls under elemental or sympathetic, as well as protection and healing, divination, and kitchen magic, clearly speaks to the complexity of Wiccan practices and belief. With spellwork, the practitioners are cultivating a deep perception of the interconnectedness of all; therefore, ethics, intent, and self-determination require emphasis. Thus, the spellwork drives Wiccans to be more active in their lives and therefore move closer to God, oneself, and the living tapestry of life. They absorb the energy that fills all around and the potential power of intent to change through the practice of magic, bathed in the beauty and depth of life.

Divination and Psychic Development

Basically, divination and psychic development are integral parts of Wiccan practice, giving practitioners an avenue through which they can remain sensitive to their intuition and seek divine guidance to explore mysteries that lie beyond the said understanding of existence. These are based on the premise that all humans intrinsically have the ability to reach out and access the energies and vibrations of the universe, which grants them a more universal view of life and the world as a whole. Wiccans embark on a very intricate spiritual path that formulates their perception of the divine as well as themselves by means of psychic powers as well as other forms of divination.

In simple terms, the activity of acquiring knowledge or guidance by using supernatural ways is called divination. Wiccans have employed a lot of instruments and techniques that draw out a unique series of views and insights. The most common types of divination include oracle card reading, scrying, pendulum dowsing, rune casting, tarot reading, and scrying. All these forms are a way of tuning in to the energies of the universe, accessing intuitive knowledge, and deciphering messages manifest as a consequence of such exchanges. The most popular usage of divination in the practice of Wicca is the tarot. Tarot is composed of Major and Minor Arcana, which are extracted from the 78 cards from a pack of cards. Tarot card readings can differ but sometimes, in daily matters and facing problems, it is called Minor Arcana while an important life event or experience contrary to spiritual learnings, it is called Major Arcana. Reading different matters or scenarios with cards enables them to understand the problems occurring in their life and to make decisions accordingly. Since every card comes with imagery and symbolism, which can be connected to any aspect of life, the readers are free to interpret it in any way suited to their own situation. People engage in a ritual that consolidates their connection to the intuitive world and spirits while shuffling the pack and drawing cards.

Another ancient form of divination currently adopted in most modern Wiccan rituals is the casting of runes. These are glyphs derived from the older alphabets, particularly Norse Futhark, to symbolize different energies, ideas, or conceptions. These glyphs are mainly used for purposes of divination by carving or drawing them on stones or wood. For example, in a rune casting, a set number of runes can be cast from a bag or container to answer an asked question. For me, that this how and meaning the runes can lay out guides practitioners toward a deeper understanding of their circumstances and of the current situation means, apart from developing intuition, that this is an invitation from practitioners to engage with knowledge so age oddly represented within symbols.

Practitioners of this very visual form of divination look for intuitive messages in scrying within a reflective surface: possibly a crystal, glass, mirror, or even the surface of water. The person who wishes to read through scrying must prepare himself or herself for a meditative state in which one's mind can quiet and open up to any impressions or visions that may occur. The gurus can look at the surface while interpreting such a scenario, and they can only see just such symbols, pictures, or messages that enlighten the ones behind their questions or concerns. Combining the conscious and unconscious self, crying allows the practitioner to dive into intuitive levels and acquire answers beyond reason. The method of Pendulum dowsing technique is easy yet powerful to understand insights and find solutions. They use a pendulum when asking yes/no questions. The most common one is the one made of crystal or other weighted object attached to a chain or string. People can read an answer by looking in what direction the pendulum swings. A pendulum that swings straight back and forth can mean a negative response, but one which sways in circular motion may mean a good response. Pendulum dowsing is a way of finding decisions; it's how to reach clarity regarding choices in life. It's very commonly used to find out options or get an inkling about a question.

The last, but far from final, extremely popular method of divination that isn't part of any of these two is oracle cards. While many are taught that tarot cards require a deep sense of the connectedness of structure which is proclaimed to make them easier to use at random chance to a novice, oracle decks differ far. Usually every card has a message, affirmation, or advice relating to a different part of life. After drawing cards from the deck, meanings are interpreted by practitioners regarding their specific queries or situations. Oracle cards are very versatile and can be used by all practitioners of every level of practice, helping them with intuitive interpretation and creative inquiry. Even though divination brings great insight and direction, psychic growth is central to developing these skills. The development of intuitive faculties forms a major part of psychic growth since it enables people to access their inner sensitivity and get information from other realms. Psychic development, used by Wiccans, is a training and an exploration devoted to the nurturing and refining of the powers of the psychic faculty that exist within each individual.

Mindfulness and meditation are the ones that shape the psyche. Continuous practice of meditation composes the mind, develops self-identification, and prepares the body for expressive revelation. Mediation is said to provide the sense of discrimination regarding differences between impulses from the intuitive self and ideas. In that sense, the individual can have a greater relationship with the inner voice, learn to trust their instinct, and know the direction they are headed. Another good strategy for psychic development is visualization. Through visualizations, practitioners can enhance their intuitive abilities and one's spiritual connectivity. For example, one may picture a white light in which they would be surrounded with a sense of safety that would guide and illuminate the situation. Visualization allows the practitioner to use their intuition to call upon the imagination and bring up a picture of something that fits the outcome desired. The adoption of visualization helps Wiccans become better at receiving messages, symbols, and insights during divination or spiritual activities.

Another good habit of the inner development practitioners is maintaining a journal. Journaling enables the practitioners to note experiences arising from dreams, divination insights, and other intuitive experiences.

People maintaining such a journal with intuitive experiences can better understand the themes, patterns, and symbols that appear in the processes. In this regard, journaling helps deepen understanding of their intuitive language as a contemplative tool to aid the practitioners in tracing their developments in every psychological dimension. Another technique for psychic ability development is intuitive exercise and practices. According to psychometry, it is helpful to practitioners; hold an object in their hands with the aim of receiving impressions or insight into its owner or history. Once people tap into the energy of an object in question, they can develop their intuitive skills and become more responsive to faint vibrations. Likewise, developing empathies and sensitivities towards the emotional states of others leads to greater awareness of energetic interactions and puts better power into the hands of practitioners to enhance psychic sensitivity.

With ongoing progression in psychic development, Wiccans may often find a desire to attend workshops or group practices. During encounters with other practitioners, they can have opportunities to share experiences and learn from one another during engagements that could sharpen intuitive functions. Group settings will motivate the practitioner to try out all aspects of his or her abilities and push their comfort zones as it opens pathways for validation and support. People collaborating at the same time will receive comments and understandings that develop their growth and knowledge about their psychic abilities. Ethics are part of psychic development and divination. It is encouraged to Wiccans that they should take these rites of paying respects to other people's right of free will with dignity. Practitioners proclaim intuitive counsel or words of divinatory insight, empowering rather than coerce and enslave, yet indeed, supporting the concept of freedom of choice. These scrying and psychic abilities have been developed to serve the betterment as ethics-based practice maintains the moral conceptions of accountability, compassion, and honesty. Furthermore, Wiccans are fully aware that prejudice has a very important role to play with regards to dealing with signs from intuition.

Bringing practical insight into psychic development and divination about intuition and reason is very crucial. Those recommended by practitioners should reflect on messages received, whether they agree with the intention and values that brought about those messages. This discernment enables people to take decisions according to both pragmatic reasons and intuitive insight; hence, one creates a sense of control over events. It speaks of a greater trend toward the intuitive and the holistic expression of spirituality. A great many people are growing to be fascinated with this practice simply because they want to uncover life's mysteries or perhaps connect with that inner wisdom lying within them. Online communities, workshops, and easy access to resources help practitioners connect with one another, share information and experiences, learn from other viewpoints, and even hone practices by doing so. Modern tools and technologies in divination and psychic development have developed generally in steps with the growth of Wicca. Apps, online courses, and other forms of digital tools are in use today to enhance the knowledge and abilities of many practitioners. These contemporary tools allow self-paced learning as they give people a chance to delve into their interests and develop themselves according to lifestyle. This fusion of ancient traditions with modern technology shows the dynamic state of Wiccan belief and how it is ever-changing. Divination and psychic development, in a nutshell, provide an indispensable ingredient in the practice of Wiccans themselves by essentially offering them a means to commune with their inner self, seek guidance, and discover life's hidden mysteries.

In a myriad of divination arts, the Wiccans channel the universe's energy and reveal vision that helps them make better spiritual pursuits. In such arts, the development of the psychic powers amplifies their effectiveness and allows a deeper understanding of the interrelation and self. Ethical values and judgment control the practices of all involved in both divination and psychic arts as these practices keep them responsible and truthful to the activities. Therefore, this timeless wisdom and input that accompanies these practices are embracing arms of Wiccans since psychic development and interest in divination are on the rise that encourages one to touch themselves and stretch into the vast tapestry of reality. With this, Wiccans can rejoice in the richness and beauty of a spiritual path because it enhances their bond with the divine and the world around through the divination process and the psychic development journey.

Wiccans contribute to a broader understanding of the spirit in the modern world; the practitioners themselves, however, consciously choose to remain true to ancient traditions but carve new pathways to resonance with contemporary needs and experiences. This manner, divination as well as psychic development serves as a bridge connecting the past to the present insofar as it guides the Wiccans on their quest of realizing a spiritual vision further interacting with the cosmos at a deeper level.

CONCLUSION

At the very end of "Exploring Wicca: From the Cauldron to the Altar: Understanding the Beliefs and Practices of Wicca," it is clear that Wicca is a way of life more in tune with nature and the divine than it is a religion or ritualistic practice.

We have read in this book about the rich history of Wicca and learned its core tenets, plus identified the rituals shaping contemporary Wiccans' lives. Whether novice Wiccans or practicing for years, there are endless chances for self-power development and attachment.

Fundamentally, Wicca asks us to listen for the cycles of life and its rhythms, honor those rhythms, and keep a close rapport with the spiritual forces surrounding us. This rich tapestry encompasses God and Goddess, elements, and natural world-innate magical properties.

Remember, this is an extremely personalized journey as you assimilate the knowledge within each of these pages into your life. Use that which resonates with you, vary your rituals to your own style of practice, and always trust your instincts. From the cauldron to the altar, from the earth beneath your feet to the celestial bodies above, Wicca will give you a most powerful route to spiritual fulfillment and a journey of self-discovery. God bless you.

Thank you for buying and reading/ listening to our book. If you found this book useful/ helpful please take a few minutes and leave a review on the platform where you purchased our book. Your feedback matters greatly to us.